GOD
and the
SELF

**Insights from Major Thinkers
in the Western
Philosophical Tradition**

D. Pulane Lucas, PhD

Archway Publishing books may be ordered through booksellers or by contacting:

Archway Publishing
1663 Liberty Drive
Bloomington, IN 47403
www.archwaypublishing.com
1 (888) 242-5904

Because of the dynamic nature of the Internet, any web addresses or links contained in this book may have changed since publication and may no longer be valid. The views expressed in this work are solely those of the author and do not necessarily reflect the views of the publisher, and the publisher hereby disclaims any responsibility for them.

Any people depicted in stock imagery provided by Thinkstock are models, and such images are being used for illustrative purposes only. Certain stock imagery © Thinkstock.

ISBN: 978-1-4808-5243-3 (sc)
ISBN: 978-1-4808-5242-6 (e)

Library of Congress Control Number: 2017954008

Print information available on the last page.

Archway Publishing rev. date: 03/07/2018

Knowledge is power.
Knowledge about yourself is self-empowerment.

~ Dr. Joe Dispenza

This book is dedicated to
my blessed and beloved son,
Stanley.

Contents

Book 3: Self-Awareness

Acknowledgments

*F*OR MANY YEARS, I have been called to compile this book; but it was not until I embarked on a day of silence that it manifested. For twenty-four hours, I committed myself to silence, prayer, and meditation. I had no communication with anyone—no face-to-face conversations, telephone, e-mail, texting, or Internet. There was also no television, radio, newspapers, magazines, or music. My objective was to remove all resistance so that I could better align myself with the will of God. I also sought to make space for the miraculous to manifest in my life. This book emerged from my day of silence.

Numerous individuals have contributed to the glorious unfolding and wonderful evolution of my life. For each of you, I am eternally grateful. While I may not mention your name in this preface, please know that you are forever in my heart and prayers.

I especially want to recognize the following individuals who had a role—large or small, intentional or unintentional—in the manifestation of this book. First, I am overwhelmed and humbled by the unconditional love that flows to me from my son, Stanley T. Wilson II. Thank you so much for introducing me to Abraham-Hicks and suggesting that I take a day of silence. I thank God for you daily. I also thank God for my handsome and loving husband,

Rev. Dr. Fred A. Lucas Jr., senior pastor of Brooklyn Community Church (BCC). Not only are we soulmates, we are blessed to be the parents of a beautiful and brilliantly talented daughter, Fredericka Lucas. Fredericka, you bring us so much joy! Thank you for the photo used for the cover of this book. God has shined His light on me and blessed me to be a stepmother to three tremendously gifted children. Thank you, Fred and Bishop Dr. Barbara E. Austin Lucas for being the parents of Prophetess Dr. Kemba Jarena Lucas, Dr. Hakim Lucas, and Kareem M. Lucas. Their accomplishments are admirable and commitment to giving back commendable. I also am grateful for our beautiful granddaughter, "Bre". All of my children have contributed to the fullness of God's blessings in my life.

I am blessed to be the daughter of wonderful, Christian parents, Delbert and Deanna Evans. I cherish your love, support, and prayers. To my siblings, Dr. Darna Hughes, Dareria Evans Pritchett, and Delbert Evans, Jr., I thank God every day for you and send each of you my love. To Stanley T. Wilson, Sr., I am grateful to God for our friendship and your presence in our son's life. May God continue to bless you and your lovely family. To the late Henry A. Wilson, Sr. and his wife, Beverly Wilson, your strength and faith in God have provided a model for Stanley, Jr., and me. I am grateful for your presence in my life. Thank you, Drs. Preston and Connie Williams, for being wonderful advisors, mentors, friends, family, and for serving as Fredericka's surrogate grandparents. Your love is unconditional and deeply appreciated.

To my awesome sisters-in-law, Dr. Patricia Mansfield and Myrna Lucas Perry: What a blessing both of you have been in my life! I cherish your love and support. My sister-friend, Anita Blake, you are one of the most beautiful women I know. You are a masterful prayer warrior, and I am honored that you are my friend. To the women of the BCC Sisterhood: Thank you for the power of your prayers, the strength of your commitment to BCC, and your love for Rev. Fred, our family, and me.

I am deeply grateful for everyone who has contributed to my academic and professional development. Fond memories abound as I reminisce about the times that I spent studying at the College of Alameda, California State University, Hayward; Harvard University; and Virginia Commonwealth University (VCU). The opportunities that were afforded to me for personal growth and professional development were immeasurable. I remain in awe of the love and support that I continue to receive at VCU and J. Sargeant Reynolds Community College. Special thanks go out to Wally R. Smith, MD, Florence Neal Cooper Smith Professor of Sickle-Cell Disease, VCU School of Medicine; David J. Barrish, MPA, CHA, Dean of Reynolds School of Business; and my dear friend and colleague Beverly B. Davis, Associate Professor and Program Head of Business Administration, Management, and Marketing.

My family and I are tremendously grateful for the prayers, support, and kind words received from our church families. I send my love to everyone at Brooklyn Community Church; Fifth Baptist Church in Richmond, VA, under the leadership of the Rev. Dr. Earl M. Brown and Rev. Ricardo L. Brown; and Union Baptist Church where the Rev. Dr. Robert W. Perry serves as senior pastor.

Finally, I deeply appreciate the support and assistance with the production of this book provided by the Archway Editorial Department and Publishing teams. Thank you for helping me create a book that is professionally edited, well-constructed, and beautifully designed. Your commitment to excellence is astounding!

I am forever humbled by the miraculous ways that God moves in my life. Love, peace, and blessings!

Preface

ON SUNDAY, FEBRUARY 26, 2017, Harvard Divinity School (HDS) professor Richard Reinhold Niebuhr, Hollis Professor of Divinity Emeritus, passed away at the age of ninety. Dr. Niebuhr was a renowned theologian, researcher, and scholar. I was blessed to have taken several of his courses during my time at the HDS during the 1990s. Much of the work in this book was written as essays or papers in Dr. Niebuhr's courses. Two courses that immersed students in the works of Kant, Schleiermacher, Coleridge, James, and others are Studies in Religion & Culture: Kant, Coleridge & Schleiermacher and a seminar on American Pragmatism. This book is a tribute to Professor Niebuhr and the knowledge and insight I acquired while taking his courses.

In addition to this book being informed by my studies with Professor Niebuhr, it also is compiled from works written during my studies in courses: Erasmus, Hume, Schopenhauer, and Royce, taught by Professor Cornel West, and Autonomy and Alienation, taught by Professor Frederick Neuhouser.

I am grateful for the time I studied religion, theology, and philosophy at HDS and while a student in the Harvard Graduate School of Arts and Science (GSAS). I enjoyed tremendously having the opportunity to work with Dr. Preston N. Williams and others on developing the Summer Leadership Institute. Since moving on from Harvard University, my teaching interests have focused primarily on business and management courses and my research on program evaluation and assessment, and public and health policy, primarily on disruptive innovation in the health care industry. I love analyzing statistical data that gives insight into organizational change, utilization trends, and policy shifts. Yet, I appreciate my exposure to religious, theological, and philosophical studies at HDS and GSAS, as well as the enlightenment I experienced and the memories cherished from my time at Harvard. This book has been waiting years for manifestation, and its time has come.

In this book, I explore the complex notions of God and the self. The book is divided into three sections. Book 1 is titled "Freedom, Guilt, and the Moral Law" and analyzes the works of Immanuel Kant (1724–1804), Samuel Taylor Coleridge (1772–1834), and Friedrich Nietzsche (1844–1900). Book 2 is titled "Dimensions of God and the Self" and examines René Descartes (1596–1650), John Locke (1632–1704), David Hume (1711–1776), Immanuel Kant (1724–1804), and Friedrich Schleiermacher (1768–1834). Book 3: "Self-Awareness" explores the self from more pragmatic perspectives and draws upon the work of William James (1842–1910).

The philosophers featured in this work, gave careful consideration to how we come to understand conceptions of God and the self. They understood their roles in the unfolding of life and making of history. They were in partnership with God. The philosophers thought and wrote during periods of religious and political upheaval. Free thinking had been repressed by the church, state, and academy; yet, dominant and oppressive religious forces were beginning to be marginalized in society. With desacralization, there were shifts toward religious liberty, cultural tolerance, individual rights, equality, human will and agency, self-fulfillment, and the cultivation of direct relationships with God. Greater emphasis was placed on the power of the human mind. Human knowledge was derived from critical thought and individual experience, and it was believed that God and humanity were moving toward perfection through a process of co-creation.

Their intellectual endeavors continue to have relevance for us today. By caring about our thoughts and actions, and being intentional about how and what we perceive, what we give our attention to, and our choices, habits, and dispositions; we can change our lives for the better. It is through our partnership with God that we manifest our own reality, lives, and history.

The study of philosophy can improve our abilities to self-reflect, imagine, and create. Thinking analytically, critically, and creatively about ourselves, ideas, concepts, and constructs helps us reassess the underlying assumptions of our beliefs, stimulate the generation of new ideas and thought patterns, and bolster problem solving skills for better decision-making and solution identification.

My aims in writing *God and the Self* are to bring forth a deepening of our understanding of and appreciation for the works and thoughts of the featured philosophers and also to encourage a more disciplined understanding of ourselves. On one hand, *God and the Self* is a handbook that assembles and examines important works from major thinkers in the Western philosophical tradition for contemporary scholarly and non-academic audiences. It illustrates how a variety of influences shape ideas. The book places the theories and intellectual projects of philosophers in relation to one another and within social and historical context. On the other hand, *God and the Self* is a guide to self-health that is written and designed to assist the reader in becoming more cognizant of his or her thoughts, while also improving the ability to be more cognitively flexible as he or she examines notions of God and the self from a variety of perspectives. It is my hope that the essays in this book enlighten the reader who is seeking an awakening and personal fulfillment. It is my prayer that the essays in this book motivate the reader who is stifled by fear, resentment, guilt, and shame to move beyond negative thought patterns to a place of hope and self-worth. My desire is that *God and the Self* engenders a revaluation of unhealthy thoughts about past experiences and inspires the reader to shift his or her perspectives toward an enlightened vision of the future based on greater self-appreciation and personal well-being.

Book 1
FREEDOM, GUILT, AND THE MORAL LAW

1

Context: The Age of Enlightenment and Spirit of Romanticism

THE PHILOSOPHERS AND THEOLOGIANS mentioned in this book are major thinkers of the Enlightenment and Romantic movements. In the eighteenth century, the convergence of a myriad of ideological, scientific, cultural, religious, and political forces gave rise to two streams of thought or general understandings of human existence. These approaches are captured in the Age of Enlightenment and the Spirit of Romanticism. In a sense, it can be said that Romanticism emerges out of and in response to Enlightenment philosophy. Romantic thinkers advocate and express many views suppressed by Enlightenment philosophers. While on the one hand, these two streams of thought are ideologically opposed to one another, on the other hand, out of the interplay between the streams of thought similarities emerge.

First, a discussion of the similarities: because both schools of thought are birthed from a common source—the minds of men—they inevitably lead to some common features. Both Enlightenment philosophy and Romanticism focus on the nature and innate powers of human beings. They each tap into the hidden essence of human nature and rise in response to oppressive human conditions (structural and traditional). Both examine aspects of man's impact on culture, history, and his environment. Both seek to liberate humanity from bondage and restrictions, to allow human beings to experience freedom.

Yet, beneath these similarities are differences. The Age of Enlightenment stresses the scientific mind. It focuses on theory, empiricism, and observation of objects. Based in reason, it elevates the rational intellect. As reason searched for commonality and unity, it made itself known in law—civil laws, moral laws, and laws of nature. Enlightenment philosophers call for the suppression of the emotions and the passions. To realize social and political progress, stability, and order, Enlightenment thinkers advocate for equality and the submission of personal will to the higher or general will.

Conversely, the Spirit of Romanticism seeks to liberate the soul. It stresses spontaneity, imagination, spirituality, and creativity. It is willing to soar to new heights of beauty, happiness, and goodness, while also entertaining magic, the bizarre and dreaded, and unsettling imagery. The unlimited reach of Romanticism seeks newer heights and lower depths of the experiences of man. Romantic philosophers look deep into the mysteries and revelations of the mind and spirit respectively. They dive into the depths of the human soul, to examine evil and death. Yet, they rise to experience unmatched feelings of love and passion. As Romantic philosophers search for social and political understanding, they advocate diversity and difference and emphasize the uniqueness of national character.

Nevertheless, both Enlightenment philosophy and Romanticism seek to liberate man from oppressive conditions, thus hoping to realize a state of freedom. Ironically, both ideologies tend to oppress. For the Enlightenment thinkers, the subjugation usually falls upon those lacking virtue, the unreasonable, and the irrational. In other words, those who threaten stability and order. The inclination of the Romantics, on the other hand, is to subjugate those who are too different: the exotic or the impure.

In summary, both the Age of Enlightenment and the Spirit of Romanticism mirror different aspects of the nature of man. They express features of the human experience, therefore contributing to our understanding of human knowledge. However, these diametrically opposed philosophies are based on human characteristics that merely reflect the paradoxical nature of man. Thus, they rise out of the same tension they seek to solve and ultimately end up contributing to.

2

Kant and the Philosophical Problem of the Knowledge of Freedom

/N THIS ESSAY, I seek to illuminate the philosophical problem embedded in the *knowledge* of freedom, as presented in Kant's *The Critique of Pure Reason*. Recognition of the weaknesses in understanding the concept of freedom is important to conceptualizing adequately the notion of freedom; otherwise, broader negative social implications are inevitable. The philosophical problem of understanding freedom, according to German Philosopher Immanuel Kant (1724 – 1804), lies in the misperception of freedom as a thing in itself. Thus, I will examine the failure to properly conceptualize freedom and reveal how the concept of freedom is comprised of equally reciprocal and opposing parts (i.e., its presence and absence) that are in dynamic tension with one another.

The paper will proceed as follows. First, I present a historical sketch of the time in which Kant wrote. The sketch places Kant's philosophical views within context. Second, I provide a theoretical framework for insight into the discussion of Kant's philosophical problem of the *knowledge* of freedom. Third, I offer an analysis of Kant's resolution of the problem of understanding freedom. Fourth, I explain the process by which Kant arrives at the "concept" of human freedom as having "objective reality." Finally, I provide a brief explanation of Kant's meaning of the consciousness of the moral law as "a fact of [pure] reason" before offering concluding remarks.

The Age of Enlightenment rose out of a myriad of intermingled events; extreme demographic shifts; economic, political, and social crises; and the convergence and divergence of religious, scientific, and philosophical ideologies. These broad transformative forces rapidly spread across seventeenth- and eighteenth- century Europe (Tarnas 1991). Wars and social upheavals ultimately led to a reconstruction of medieval European society. It was in the center of these vast changes, as well as under the rule of the enlightened despot Frederick the Great of Prussia that Kant thought and wrote (Palmer and Colton 1995).

Kant's thoughts were heavily influenced by philosophers like David Hume and John Locke, (Tarnas 1991). Jean-Jacques Rousseau, who wrote about how irrational, self-destructive human urges and oppressive social institutions restricted human freedom and man's ability to act morally (Mandt 1990; Palmer and Colton 1995), also had a significant impact on Kant's thoughts. Hence, in the *Critique of Pure Reason*, Kant provides a critique of theoretical reason[1] and addresses the issue of freedom and rationality.[2] Kant also sought to answer how synthetic a priori propositions are possible and true. He realized that all knowledge arises in experience, but not all knowledge is derived from experience, because of the limitations of reason.[3] Kant concludes that synthetic a priori propositions are possible and true through his "Copernican Revolution," (Beck 1960, 21).[4]

Kant maintains that objects cannot be objects of knowledge unless they come from sense experience and are subjected to certain a priori conditions—those prior to or independent of experience—in the human mind. Thus, objects of our knowledge, those coming from sense experience, are all phenomena.[5] They are not noumena or things in themselves (Staloff 1992). Therefore, says Kant, we can never experience the world as it is; we can only experience the world through our own representation of it. This leads to Kant's metaphysical distinction between noumena and phenomena (Staloff 1992).

For Kant, human knowledge is sense data combined with forms and understanding, a process unique to humans. The forms of understanding are called transcendental logic (Staloff 1992; Kant [1781] 1990), which interfaces with a priori concepts that are necessary conditions for an object to be thought. See exhibit 1 for a table of Kant's categories of judgments (Kant [1781] 1990). The *"quality of judgments"* is comprised of affirmative, negative, and infinite. These a priori concepts help theoretically illustrate Kant's processes of cognitive synthesis and transcendental logic. The "infinite" reality "must be distinguished from affirmative judgments," through the process of juxtaposing negative judgments (Kant [1781] 1990, 57).

In reference to freedom and transcendental logic, Kant might state, "Freedom is not determinism." (In other words, to know what freedom is, one must know what it is not.) This statement is a negative judgment and in its logical form actually affirms because it locates freedom in the unlimited realm of independence (Kant [1781] 1990). Given "the whole sphere of possible existences," Kant would hold that our notion of freedom is comprised of both elements of determinism and independence (57). Our theoretical understanding of every concept, notion, or idea requires that our minds dynamically hold thoughts of their presence and absence simultaneously.

Kant also segments his table of categories (see exhibit 2 for table) into four sections, corresponding with his table of judgments. Each section is composed of three classes: sensibility/intuition, concepts/understanding, and a third resulting from a synthesis of the first two. Thus, the table "contains all the elementary conceptions of the understanding," (Kant [1781] 1990, 64). In reference to Kant's "category of *quality*" that is comprised of reality, negation, and limitation, he explains that "Limitation is merely Reality conjoined with Negation," (65). Kant clarifies that Negation, an element of the second category, is not merely a deduction of the other two but "a primitive conception of the pure understanding" (65). As human beings, we come to know every concept, notion, or idea not only by its presence or reality, but by its absence or negation, and also by our ability to distinguish the boundaries between presence and absence, known as limitation.

How do Kant's categories and judgments specifically relate to the problem of the knowledge of freedom? By placing the concept of freedom within Kant's theoretical analysis of categories and judgments, our understanding of freedom is conceptualized as a complete idea. However, prior to cognition, freedom is comprised of several unsubordinated, noncausal, equally reciprocal opposing parts. Thus, to conceive of freedom, its component parts of determinism and independence are represented in "the diversity of pure intuition" (Kant [1781] 1990, 65). "[T]he synthesis of this diversity" manifests itself into the moral law, i.e., freedom (independence) under a self-imposed law (determinism) according to one's nature. Cognition of freedom only surfaces after the "necessary synthetical unity" of concepts, and judgments are performed (65). Ironically, tension between independence and determinism arises; creating an antinomy or contradiction (Beck 1960) in the relationship of freedom and our ability to understand it (Kant [1781] 1990). Reason itself is the culprit as it attempts to reveal freedom as a transcendental notion rising from the idea of causality (Beck 1960).

When examining freedom within the context of Kant's "Categories," we see the equivalent parts of freedom (independence/thesis and determinism/antithesis) as forces that keep one another in check. With his "Judgments," independence cannot be understood or even exist without reference to determinism; thus, this subtle association binds them together. Thus, when one thinks of the presence of independence, one cannot help but also think of its absence— in other words, determinism. Yet, the process of understanding, the forces that balance the categories, and the tension that binds the judgments may confuse the cognition of objects. To solve the antinomy, Kant recommends "transcendental reflection"[6] that takes us to the transcendental dialectic,[7] the parting of the world into two distinct realms, the noumenal and the phenomenal. By "showing that the thesis can be applied to the relationship between noumena … and phenomena, and the antithesis is restricted to relations among phenomena" (Beck 1960, 26), Kant overcomes his philosophical problem.

Categories, which form sense data, apply only to the phenomena. Objects that go beyond the realm of phenomena exist in the realm of noumena, that which cannot be experienced or known. It is a natural disposition of the human mind to apply the concepts transcendentally, also called the "subjective necessity."[8] It is this transposition of objects that gives rise to metaphysics. Although the transcendental dialectic does not give us any legitimate knowledge, it does have a very important regulative function in our phenomenal inquiry and actions.

Transcendental ideas, such as God, freedom, and immortality, led Kant to examine the impact of their regulative function on human behavior in the area of morality (Staloff 1992). He believed that such ideas could have practical and beneficial ramifications within society. Specifically, Kant's categorical imperative[9] was the concept that led him to his concept of human freedom as a concept of objective reality.[10] Like freedom, the categorical imperative results from the synthesis of independence and determinism. It is with the categorical imperative, a binding unconditional obligation that is not based on personal characteristics or circumstances, that Kant maintains "morality demands that we act on the sort of policies which, if adopted by everyone, would generate a community of free and equal members, each of whom in the process of realizing his own purposes also further the aims of his fellows" (Kant [1785] 1983, xv).

What does Kant mean when he says consciousness of the moral law "may be called a fact of [pure] reason"? In the section entitled "Fundamental Law of Pure Practical Reason" in the *Critique of Practical Reason*, Kant addresses the moral law as a fact of pure reason ([1788] 1993, 30–33). Kant posits that rational beings possess a will (Beck 1960),[11] "independent of empirical conditions" and "determined [a priori] by the mere form of law." Such a law, or the moral law, "forces itself upon us as a synthetic [a priori] proposition" (Kant [1788] 1993, 31). The moral law is therefore considered a "fact of pure practical reason" because "it proclaims itself as originating law" (31–32). In other words, once conscious of the moral law, a rational agent will self-legislate his or her actions independent of experience and execute the actions as duties, according to the categorical imperative.

In conclusion, Kant's understanding of the concept of freedom, theoretically and practically, rises from the social atmosphere and conditions of his time. It was amid cultural and ideological clashes, intense enlightenment and progress, and extreme poverty and oppression that he sought to tap into the innate sense of morality within humans. Kant's categorical imperative, like the metaphysical constructs of God, is a transcendental idea conceived of in part to regulate human behavior in social environments. Believing that freedom is critical for the survival of humanity, Kant posits his categorical imperative hoping that people would enact policies and laws to create social order. Kant's categorical imperative embodies Locke's thought on civil government. Locke writes in his *Second Treatise of Government*: "Where there is no law, there is no freedom" (Locke [1690] 1980, Chapter VI, Sec. 57). Kant sought to construct through reason a universal moral rule that applies to every rational agent. Kant offers an example of a categorical imperative (we may recognize this as the Golden Rule): "[D]o not do to others what you do not want done to yourself" ([1785] 1983, 37). He also believes that by willfully adhering to moral laws, humans acquire the ability to mentally and emotionally transcend their reality, awaken to their purpose, and consequently spur growth and prosperity in society.

Over the course of his lifetime, Kant's views about God and the categorical imperative evolved and conflated. He later suggested that "the moral experience *itself* may legitimately be regarded as an experience of the Divine," and "The categorical imperative ... leads directly to God [and] serves as a pledge of His reality" (Kant [1793] 1934, lxvi). In other words, Kant came to believe that "God reveals Himself" to those who adhere to the categorical imperative, and each individual finds "God ... in and through the moral law" (lxvi).

Exhibit 1 The Three Momenta of Kant's Four Categories of Judgments (Kant [1781] 1990, 56)

I.	*Quantity*:	Universal
		Particular
		Singular
II.	*Quality*:	Affirmative
		Negative
		Infinite
III.	*Relation*:	Categorical
		Hypothetical
		Disjunctive
IV.	*Modality*:	Problematical
		Assertorical
		Apodictical

Exhibit 2 Kant's Categories of the Pure Conception of Understanding (Kant [1781] 1990, 62)

I.	*Quantity*:	Unity
		Plurality
		Totality
II.	*Quality*	Reality
		Negation
		Limitation
III.	*Relation*:	Of Inherence and Subsistence (substantia et accidens)
		Of Causality and Dependence (cause and effect)
		Of Community (reciprocity between the agent and patient)
IV.	*Modality*:	Possibility-Impossibility
		Existence-Nonexistence
		Necessity-Contingence

3

The Good Will, the Highest Good, and the Kingdom of Ends

*I*N THIS ESSAY, I seek to show that the aim of Kant's moral philosophy is to counter evil on two levels: the personal and the communal. To achieve this aim, Kant sets up a threefold attack. First, he establishes that there is a good will within every human being. Second, he obligates the good will to bring forth the "perfect" highest good. Third, through the realization of the perfect highest good, he posits that there is a dual-function kingdom of ends designed to oppose evil.

Introduction

German philosopher Immanuel Kant (1724 – 1804) begins his moral philosophy with the individual and the human will. He contends that the will is the determining factor in man's disposition (Kant [1793] 1934).[12] To have a good disposition means that man has a good will. Thus, only by possessing a good will can man bring forth the "highest good" (Kant [1785] 1983, 9, [396]). Kant then moves from an analysis of individual moral behavior to the ethical conduct of the group. He claims that if each member of a group acts to bring forth the highest good, a community "of free and equal members" will emerge. In such an environment, each member realizes his or her own purpose and potential while also helping others to realize the same (Kant [1785] 1983). Kant's moral philosophy has one ultimate objective: the realization of a kingdom of ends. Kant's kingdom of ends is conceptualized to oppose evil within the individual and inside or outside of community.

To achieve the objective of this essay, I begin with a discussion of Kant's notion of a good will. I will then define the "highest good" (Kant [1785] 1983, 9, [396]) and discuss how a good will can bring forth the highest good. Next, I will illustrate how bringing forth the highest good is equivalent to acting according to the categorical imperative. Finally, I will show how Kant imagines that moral beings, acting according to the categorical imperative, can bring forth a kingdom of ends ([1785] 1983).[13]

The Good Will

Before discussing the good will, a brief introduction to Kant's notion of the "original predisposition" of man is called for (Kant [1793] 1934, 21–39).[14] Man's predisposition, according to Kant, exists in him before birth. It is "neither good nor bad"; in fact, Kant claims that man "is as much the one as the other, partly good, partly bad" ([1793] 1934, 16). The good or evil, says Kant, lies not in man's nature but in his choices that ultimately determine his disposition ([1793] 1934). Thus, having a good disposition relates directly to Kant's idea of having a *good will* (Kant [1785] 1983).

Kant maintains, "There is no possibility of thinking of anything at all in the world, or even out of it, which can be regarded as good without qualification, except a *good will*" (Kant [1785] 1983, 7, [393]). If a man has a good will, he chooses actions based on a maxim that incorporates the moral law. However, maintaining a good will is difficult because an endless array of factors, including the moral law, influence the will and determine the choices that human beings make. Thus, the good will occurs as man *continuously* makes morally based choices (Kant [1793] 1934),[15] and he remains engaged in the "endless progress[ion] ... of moral perfection" (Kant [1788] 1993, 129, [123]).

The notion of freedom is essential to having a good will. Freedom brings responsibility, thus making man accountable for his actions and disposition.[16] Man, asserts Kant, must himself be responsible for what he becomes in life. His "condition must be an effect of his free choice; for otherwise, he could not be held responsible for it and could therefore be *morally* neither good nor evil" (Kant [1793] 1934, 40). In other words, man's moral growth "begins not in the improvement of his practices but rather in the transforming of his cast of mind and in the grounding of a character" (43). "The predisposition is thus gradually transformed into a cast of mind, and *duty*, for its own sake, begins to have a noticeable importance in [man's heart]" (Kant [1793] 1934, 44), therefore, leading to the presence of a good will. Such a will is necessary to counter the bad "influences on the mind" and the evil passions within the heart (Kant [1785] 1983, 7, [393]). However, "A good will," contends Kant, "is good not because of what it effects or accomplishes, nor because of its fitness to attain some proposed end; it is good only through its willing, it is good in itself" ([1785] 1983, 7, [393]).

The Highest Good

"The establishment of a good will" is reason's highest practical function, says Kant ([1785] 1983, 9, [396]). Thus, only a rational being with a good will can bring forth the highest good. Kant acknowledges the inherent ambiguity in his notion of "the highest good" (9, [396]) and admits a lack of clarity regarding its dual nature. The "highest good" may mean the "perfect" highest good or the "supreme" highest good. The *perfect highest good* is a synthesis of virtue and happiness (i.e., happiness in proportion to virtue) (117, [111]).[17] It "is that whole which is no part of a yet larger whole of the same kind" (116, [110]). The *supreme highest good*," on the other hand, is the virtuous will (117, [111]).[18] It "is the unconditional condition, i.e., the condition which is subordinate to no other" (116, [110]). Given this clarification, moving forward in this essay, I will refer to the "highest good" as the "perfect" highest good, since it is the synthesis of virtue and proportional happiness, and best encompasses Kant's notion of the highest good.

Kant asserts that our duty is not merely to bring forth a good will but also to strive to bring forth the perfect highest good, i.e., synthesis of virtue and proportional happiness. Man, however, cannot bring forth the perfect highest good without pure practical reason. Kant writes:

> Only a rational being has the power to act according to his conception of laws, i.e., according to principles, and thereby has he a will ... [Essentially,] the will is a faculty of choosing only that which reason, independently of inclination, recognizes as being practically necessary, i.e., as good. ([1785] 1983, 23, [412])

Yet, a rational being, acting according to the moral law, but without happiness, says Kant, is unwise. He maintains that a rational being who is in "need of happiness and also worthy of it [who does not] partake of it could not be in accordance with the perfect volition of an omnipotent rational being" (Kant [1788] 1993, 117, [111]).

Bringing forth the perfect highest good requires mastery over human nature, given that man's nature is partly bad. However, man is incapable of making judgments about the ground underlying the actions of his will because of his limitations: frailty, impurity, and wickedness (Kant [1785] 1983; Kant [1793] 1934). Kant explains that it is impossible for man to know the motive upon which his acts of virtue or duty rest—even "after the keenest self-examination ... there cannot with certainty be at all inferred ... that some secret impulse of self-love, merely appearing as the idea of duty, was not the actual determining cause of the will" ([1785] 1983 19, [407]). Kant contends that humans flatter themselves with false claims to more noble motives ([1785] 1983). Yet, since man cannot know the underlying motives of his actions, Kant provides him with a practical rule as an incentive to act morally. Morality itself, then, obligates man with absolute necessity to act according to the moral law.

"Duty," says Kant, "is the necessity of an action done out of respect for the law" ([1785] 1983, 13, [400]). Such an action excludes all influences of inclination; otherwise, the act would be considered heteronomous, i.e., giving in to passion. Such a moral act is done according to the categorical imperative: "Act only by the imperative that you can at the same time will that there is a universal law" (30, [421]). It also brings forth the perfect highest good.

Kant recognizes, however, that problems arise when one attempts to universalize a maxim. Let's look at the universal moral rule "Thou shalt not kill." In his taped lecture, Michael Sugrue (1992) asks us to consider a hitman hired to kill for personal gain (e.g., money or enhanced reputation). He recognizes he is about to do an evil act. Surely, he could not wish that everyone should commit murder whenever they want to. Sugrue goes on to say that the hitman knows there is something intrinsically immoral with the act of killing. Yet, for this hit, he wants to be an exception to the rule. If the hitman were to take the maxim of his particular action "I will kill for personal gain" and universalize it, he would realize that his maxim would self-destruct. He would find that if everyone found it acceptable to kill for personal gain, respect for human life would disintegrate, and he would eventually become a victim himself.

The hitman, however, wants to live in a world where everyone else is good, where life is cherished, and where no one will murder him— but he transgresses on a duty, "Thou shalt not kill," and does the opposite of a maxim that could be universalized. He acts contrary to the moral law, taking the liberty to break it as an exception (Kant [1785] 1983, 32, [424]). The basic notion behind the categorical imperative is, however, that it is inconsistent when one cannot will that it (categorical imperative) is a universal law. Thus, the hitman fails to act according to the categorical imperative.

Such an arbitrary exception to the universal moral rule, Kant argues, is an example of succumbing to heteronomy. For Kant, when we give in to our desires, we are not free. Free behavior is rational behavior, moral behavior. Not only do we lose our freedom and behave heteronomously, we break the categorical imperative and do what we know is wrong or evil. When we follow the categorical imperative, we behave freely, rationally, and autonomously. Thus, we are taking responsibility for our actions, living up to moral rules, and realizing that there is one universal moral law. In other words, autonomy is the activity of a rational agent making a moral law that she herself obeys.

The categorical imperative has an important regulative function among autonomous beings. It provides an incentive for moral conduct and instills a sense of duty to the moral law (Kant [1793] 1934), while having positive effects not solely on individual behavior but also on group behavior. This is especially important because the perfect highest good

> cannot be achieved merely by the exertions of the single individual toward his own moral perfection, but requires rather a union of such individuals into a whole toward the same goal— into a system of well-disposed men, in which and through whose unity alone the highest moral good can come to pass—the idea of such a whole, as a universal republic based on laws of virtue, is an idea completely distinguished from all moral laws. (Kant [1793] 1934, 89)

The perfect highest good also requires an absolute whole, i.e., a community of rational beings, to bring about happiness—a portion of the highest good. Kant writes:

> the concept of happiness is such an indeterminate one that even though everyone wishes to attain [it] ... [they] can never say definitely ... what it is that [they wish] ... The reason for this is that all the elements belonging to the concept of happiness are unexceptionally empirical ... [And requires] a maximum well-being in [one's] present and in every future condition. (Kant [1785] 1983, 27, [418])

In other words, to attain a maximum well-being, individuals must encounter the other—ideas, things, concepts, and individuals—for contrast, and they must experience the other for love, support, and affirmation to manifest in their lives.

The Kingdom of Ends

Kant proclaims that a "kingdom of ends" consists of a "systematic union of different rational beings" acting "through common objective [moral] laws," (Kant [1785] 1983, 39, [433]). By this he means that rational human beings are acting to treat their own humanity and the humanity of others only as ends in themselves and never merely as means toward an end (xix). The resulting effect is a union of people coming together, free and equal, "for the self-same end," acting according to the categorical imperative. They are leading to "the establishment of a COMMONWEALTH under moral laws, as a federated and therefore [a] stronger power to withstand the assaults of the evil principle" (Kant [1793] 1934, 139).

Kant's notion of a kingdom of ends essentially has a dual function. It manifests itself in two distinct realms. On the one hand, both realms are similar in that they are charged with countering evil. On the other hand, the manner in which the realms operate is different. The first realm operates on an individual level, within the moral agent. It arises as each moral agent acts in accordance with the categorical imperative, which serves as a counter-incentive to the evil that influences man's disposition away from the good. Kant alleges that all moral acts are metaphysically housed in an abstract ideal kingdom of ends.

The second realm operates on a communal level, both within the community and as a force that emerges out of the community. It functions in the kingdom of ends, a physical community of moral individuals based on sense and experience. Its members are united rational beings, acting according to the categorical imperative, and together forming a power strong enough to counter the evil assaults in the world (Kant 1934).

In conclusion, Kant's moral philosophy seeks to counter evil on the personal and communal levels. He begins with individual morality and the good will to establish the condition to bring forth the perfect highest good. Kant then maintains that individual effort is not enough to realize the perfect highest good.[19] For Kant, individual morality is a prerequisite for the realization of the perfect highest good. Rational human beings must first personally act morally before joining a community of morally responsible beings, which is a necessity for the realization of the perfect highest good and the subsequent founding of a kingdom of ends. Kant's kingdom of ends is charged with the dual functions of challenging and conquering the evil that lurks in the human heart and that exists in the world.

4

Reflections on The Rime of the Ancient Mariner and the Appreciation of Life's Challenges

*T*HIS ESSAY OFFERS REFLECTIONS on Samuel Taylor Coleridge's *The Rime of the Ancient Mariner* (1834). I employ the poetic symbolism of Kant's Notions of Infinite Guilt and the Categorical Imperative as theoretical frameworks for interpreting and understanding Coleridge's poem.

In this piece, I assert that the mariner's transgression is a major theme of *The Rime of the Ancient Mariner*. I do this by addressing three questions: What is the mariner's transgression? Is he "guilty"? Is he free? Kant's moral philosophy forms the backdrop for my responses. Kant's work deeply influenced Coleridge (1772 – 1834), an English poet, philosopher, theologian, and literary critic (Coleridge [1817] 1975, 84). Coleridge writes: "The writings of the illustrious sage of Konigsberg, the founder of the Critical Philosophy, more than any other work at once invigorated and disciplined my understanding" (84). Coleridge undoubtedly incorporated Kantian themes and principles into *The Rime*, which he worked on from 1797 until 1816.[20] The *Grounding for the Metaphysics of Morals* and the *Religion Within the Limits of Reason Alone* laid the foundation for this essay.

In *The Rime of the Ancient Mariner*, Coleridge seeks to take the mind of his reader on an imaginative journey as he synthesizes philosophy and poetry while symbolically representing philosophical ideas. He draws upon Kant's notions that humans have limited understanding and suffer from inescapable guilt. Coleridge attempts to create Kant's categorical imperative poetically by symbolically combining absolute freedom (i.e., acting according to the moral law), with the lack of freedom associated with the burden of guilt. In this essay, I take an in-depth look at both of these propositions. The essay proceeds as follows. After an examination of the mariner's transgression and the accompanying guilt, I offer an explanation of the implications of the guilt. I will then discuss whether or not the mariner is free and finally provide summary comments.

The Rime of the Ancient Mariner begins with Coleridge telling a story of how a mariner sets sail on the open sea (Coleridge 1957, 38). The sea, with its vast open space, metaphorically represents freedom. Here, Coleridge draws upon Kant's notion of freedom. For Kant, however, freedom brings responsibility, thus, making man accountable for his actions, disposition, and character (Kant [1793] 1934, 40).[21] In an essay titled "The Ethical Significance of Kant's Religion," John R. Silber explains Kant's notion of human freedom and responsibility:

> The moral individual makes himself into whatever he is from a moral standpoint. He acquires his own virtues and vice through his own free actions. Others may force him to act contrary to the moral law, but no one can make him violate it. (Kant [1793] 1934, cxxxi)

As the mariner sails into the unknown, he is challenged to make character-defining decisions. Kant admits that continuously making good choices that lead to a good disposition is not easy (Kant [1793] 1934, 43).[22] Coleridge, therefore, seeks to reveal the tension that free human beings encounter through the mariner's struggles (e.g., the shooting of the albatross, the weather, the death of shipmates, and loneliness). The mariner's primary transgression is the killing of the albatross. Thus, the inhospitable killing of "the pious bird of good omen" is an assault on "the good" (Coleridge 1957, 40).

This act of evil is not the real enemy, says Kant; the real enemy is deeper within the nature of man's will, lodged not in man's inclinations, "but in his perverted maxim, and so in freedom itself" (Kant [1793] 1934, 50–51).

> Those inclinations merely make difficult the *execution* of the good maxim that opposes them; whereas genuine evil consists in this, that a man does not *will* to withstand those inclinations when they tempt him to transgress—so it is really the disposition of failing to counter evil that is the true enemy (50–51).

Kant maintains, "Man's moral growth of necessity begins not in the improvement of his practices but rather in the transforming of his cast of mind and in the grounding of a character" (Kant [1793] 1934, 43). Man, therefore, begins to act out of duty for duty's sake.[23] If the transformation of man's character is essential to his moral development, why does Coleridge fail to reveal the mariner's intention in shooting the albatross? We are not given even the slightest hint whether the killing was out of duty or not.

Coleridge deliberately leaves the reader uncertain. He seeks to capture and heighten the reader's sense of ambivalence. In doing this, Coleridge attempts to explore a Kantian theme by poetically embodying the theme. Kant explains that there is moral uncertainty associated with all human action (Kant [1785] 1983 19). Thus, Coleridge allows the reader to experience—through the telling of *The Rime* and the activation of the imagination—the uncertainty that he or she would otherwise feel if the reader were to analyze the intentions of his or her own actions. Kant explains it is impossible to determine if an act is "in accordance with what duty commands." "There are always doubts as to whether what occurred has really been done from duty and [whether it] has moral worth" (19, [406]).

Coleridge, like Kant, understands that the impurity of human nature may cause man secretly to disguise self-interest behind the idea of duty. Thus, Coleridge leaves the reader vacillating over the albatross's death, because the mariner himself cannot know the true intentions of his actions. Kant maintains, "[w]e like to flatter ourselves with the false claim to a more noble motive; but in fact we can never, even by the strictest examination, completely plumb the depths of the secret incentives of our actions" (Kant [1785] 1983, 19, [407]).[24] For Coleridge, to regard highly the mariner's apparently thoughtless shooting of the bird would be what Kant asserts as *wisdom* called out against *folly*. In other words, wisdom allows itself

> to be deceived by inclinations through mere carelessness, instead of summoning itself (wisdom) against *wickedness* (the wickedness of the human heart), which secretly undermines the disposition with soul-destroying principles (Kant [1793] 1934, 50).

In essence, the killing of the albatross represents an assault on "the good," which violates the moral law.[25] Given the mariner's transgression and the fact that he is unable to assess the intentions of his act, "how is [he] to gain absolution from the guilt that follows from the impurity and weakness of his will?" (Kant [1793] 1934, cxxxii). How does a man who has transformed his cast of mind[26] deal with the guilt of his past transgression? Here Coleridge draws upon Kant's discussion of guilt and grace; however, Kant himself vacillates on this issue.[27] "There is neither antinomy nor resolution," Silber explains about Kant's position.

> [Kant's] absolute conception of freedom precludes the need for grace, since every guilty man freely wills to become guilty; the purity of the moral law precludes the granting of grace, for grace violates the uncompromising nature of the law ([1793] 1934, cxxxii).

Writes John R. Silber: "In order to make sense of the idea of personal responsibility, Kant argue[s] that freedom is absolute. Yet by holding that man's responsibility is absolute, he condemned man to an insufferable burden of guilt" (Kant [1793] 1934, cxxxiii). For Kant, "if a man is guilty, it is his own fault, and he must bear the full and non-transferable burden" (cxxxi). Guilt, says Kant, is infinite (66).[28]

> Whatever a man may have done in the way of adopting a good disposition, and indeed, however steadfastly he may have persevered in conduct conformable to such a disposition, he *nevertheless started from evil*, and this debt he can by no possibility wipe out. (Kant [1793] 1934, 66)

Essentially, guilt cannot be relieved through grace or atonement. Kant writes that such sins are "*the most personal of all debts*," and "only the culprit can bear" no matter how "magnanimous" another may be and "wish to take [the debt] upon himself for the sake of" the transgressor (Kant [1793] 1934, 66). Kant explains:

> The extent of this guilt is due not so much to the
> *infinitude* of the Supreme Lawgiver whose authority
> is thereby violated (for we understand nothing
> of such transcendent relationships of man to the
> Supreme Being) as to the fact that this moral evil
> lies in the *disposition* and the maxims in general, in
> *universal basic principles* rather than in particular
> transgressions. (Kant [1793] 1934, 66)

For Kant, "all men seem to find themselves guilty" (Kant [1793] 1934, cxxxiii).

Is the mariner free? Ironically, the answer is no and yes. How can this be, when Coleridge writes, "And ever and anon throughout [the mariner's] future life **an agony constraineth him** to travel from land to land" (Coleridge 1957, 54–55, emphasis mine)?[29] It would appear that this constraint would lead one to answer the question with a categorical *no*. Coleridge reveals that the mariner, who represents all human beings, is trapped in Kant's inescapable cycle of guilt. The poem itself embodies this endless loop as the reader is led back to its beginning upon its conclusion. Thus, if the mariner is obligated to remain within the cycle of guilt, how can he also be free?

With *The Rime*, Coleridge attempts to represent poetically Kant's categorical imperative. He does this by establishing freedom as the mariner sailing on the open sea; yet, he morally obligates (unconditionally and with absolute necessity because Coleridge is the creator of the poem) the mariner to tell his tale. By subjecting the mariner repeatedly to telling his story, Coleridge lyrically and poetically synthesizes freedom and guilt (lack of freedom) and therefore philosophically embraces and embodies freedom under the law, i.e., the categorical imperative. In other words, the mariner submits his will to the moral law and therefore becomes an autonomous being (Kant [1785] 1983, 41).[30] Kant writes: "Now this is precisely the formula of the categorical imperative and is the principle of morality. Thus a free will and a will subject to moral law are one and the same" (49, [447]).[31]

In summary, Coleridge beautifully captures Kant's categorical imperative in *The Rime of the Ancient Mariner*. However, he falls short in two areas—the first with Kant, the second with philosophy. The first shortcoming has to do with the categorical imperative and the notion of not using others as a means. To address the mariner's guilt, Coleridge requires the mariner to interfere with and impede the lives of others with his never-ending storytelling. For Kant, a feature of the categorical imperative is that one cannot use another person as merely a means to an end. We must respect the humanity of others as ends in themselves. Clearly, the wedding guest's response of foregoing his plans to listen to the mariner recount events cannot represent the response of others. Not everyone is willing to hear the mariner's tale (except in *The Rime*). Thus, Coleridge has either openly violated an essential principle of the categorical imperative, or he seeks to illustrate that human beings, all of whom have guilt, cannot escape using others as means because we are all part of the whole, humankind.

The second challenge to Coleridge's poem arises from his attempt to represent a philosophical idea. In an essay titled "Philosophy as Literature," Lewis White Beck addresses the tension between philosophy and poetry: "At the end of the *Republic*, Plato recounts the 'ancient quarrel between philosophy and poetry' and banishes the poet from the ideal city because the poet may mislead the citizen by the sweetness of his song" (Beck 1980, 235). Coleridge also has made "illusion attractive, [thereby taking] the mind away from truth, the realm of the philosopher" (235–36). Although Coleridge effectively piques the imagination with his tale of the ancient mariner, his attempt to synthesize philosophy and poetry runs the risk of losing the reader in imagery and his bizarre story, thus, causing the reader to miss the philosophical truth embedded in the poem.

Finally, Coleridge's restrictions upon the mariner's life without protest, his presentation of the mariner's transgression without elaborating on its underlying conflict, and the mariner's endless telling of his tale without rejection fail to capture fully and highlight explicitly the Kantian notion of "experience requiring resistance." This idea is revealed in the following passage, one where Kant himself synthesizes philosophy and poetry: "The light dove, cleaving the air in her free flight, and feeling its resistance, might imagine that its flight would be still easier in empty space."[32]

The dove might imagine that her flight would be easier without the resistance of the wind against her body and wings. Such a tension-free flight, however, is not possible. Resistance is a necessary condition for her free flight.

Coleridge's life was filled with the beauty of "the practice and love of poetry" (Warren 1969, 25). Yet, he imagined a life without the guilt (resistance) associated with the turmoil of the opium addiction that had devastated his life. He

> lived into the guilt of opium long before the Mariner shot the Albatross: he knew [inescapable] guilt … and … longed for a view of the universe which would absolve him of responsibility and

comfort him with the thought of participation.
(Warren 1969, 25)

Coleridge's soul was in endless agony, and he condemned the mariner to a similar fate with an addiction to eternal storytelling that consumes the mariner's life and impedes his freedom. The mariner is unable to exercise his free will. He loses the ability to make choices about the direction of his life and the ability to determine his own future. Although *The Rime of the Ancient Mariner* may subtly conceal this tension, Coleridge himself had intimate knowledge with losing control of his life and of living with guilt. Like the mariner, Coleridge also accepts this fate.

Through a reading of Coleridge's background and writings, we gain great appreciation for the challenges he faced in his life. And yet, his struggles created opportunities for the emergence of purpose, genius, and greatness. I can only imagine that Coleridge, the theologian, never lost faith in God. He, like the mariner, knew that things would ultimately work out for his good.

It is through our struggles with resistance (i.e., guilt, shame, fear, and resentment) that we clarify our desires and purpose in life. And, like the dove thrusting forward in flight and not looking back, we too must have faith and continue to move forward in life, understanding that resistance can help give life direction. Resistance causes us to self-reflect, and consequently to want and ask for wellbeing, self-worth, joy and happiness, freedom, and abundance. As human beings, we are endowed with the abilities to image and create—the ability to turn thoughts to things. Many of our most significant manifestations emerge from contrasts, which are necessary for the glorious expansion of life and the universe (Hicks and Hicks 2009).

5

Nietzsche's Revaluation of Morals

IN THIS ESSAY, I argue that the aim of Nietzsche's critique of Christianity is not solely to assess the conventional moral system and bring forth a revaluation of morals; he seeks a radical alteration in the behavior of humans. Friedrich Nietzsche (1844 – 1900), German philosopher and cultural critic, believes that a transformation of the moral fiber of society, from passivity to assertion, will consequently ignite within humans a "will to power." To accomplish this, he seeks to eradicate "slave morality" from society and establish a new set of morals that resembles—without being identical to—those of the warrior elite of ancient times. According to Nietzsche, slave morality or Christianity has come to dominate the Western world, which he considers its major weakness because of the inherent illness of guilt. Nietzsche maintains that guilt entered the world through self-conscious individuals. Guilt was inspired within these individuals, according to Nietzsche, because they were unable to fulfill their obligation in a contractual agreement with God that was based on a creditor-debtor relationship.

In addition to the internalized punishment of guilt, Nietzsche wants to go beyond Christianity because of the accompanying alienation and hatred of natural instincts that arise within humans. Nietzsche essentially believes that he is a liberator, out to eradicate the negative effects of slave morality, while returning to the best of noble morality. This new combination of morals will create a society where humans can escape the burden of guilt and unleash their true genius.

The essay proceeds as follows. First, it presents an outline of the origins of the value judgments of "good and bad" and "good and evil." An understanding of Nietzsche's views on the origins of good and evil is crucial, specifically because it sheds light on the distinctions between his beliefs about slave morality and those of traditional Christianity. Second, it provides a discussion of Nietzsche's critique of slave morality and noble morality. This discussion focuses on the characteristic shifts that occurred in the transition from one type of moral system to another. Third, it offers an explanation of why Nietzsche wishes to supplant slave morality. Here, I explain his reasons for seeking to instill in society a new type of morality that combines attributes from both slaves and nobles. This discussion appears within a Christian theological framework and explores Nietzsche's claims on the positive and negative aspects of guilt.

Nietzsche ([1887] 1967, 27) holds that moral categories of good and evil, i.e., slave morality, replaced the noble mode of valuation based on good and bad. This "conceptual transformation" occurred with a shift in the way certain humans valued themselves in relation to others. The word "good," derived from nobles, implied the actions and attributes associated with the higher class (26). As the meaning of good evolved, it came to mean "pure," "blond-headed," and "having a soul of higher order." In contradistinction, "bad" represented "impurity," "dark-skinned," "dark-haired," and the slaves or common people with poor souls (30). The quality of the soul eventually became connected to the kind of person one was, and the illusion emerged that if one was good or bad, he or she was responsible for his or her condition.

The Jews, who were oppressed under Roman rule, however, inverted the noble mode of valuation, Nietzsche argues. Thus, there was the movement from the nobles being good, powerful, beautiful, and beloved by God to the idea that "the wretched alone are the good; the poor, impotent, lowly alone are the good; the suffering, deprived, sick, ugly alone are pious, alone are blessed by God" ([1887] 1967, 34). Nietzsche claims that the inversion, the slave revolt in morality, brought about the concepts of good and evil. A new kind of love blossomed from this reversal, one in which Jesus "brought blessedness and victory to the poor" (35). Nietzsche admits that slave morality triumphed over *nobler* ideals, and consequently, the common person won.

The inversion of the moral system from noble to slave-based morality caused two fundamental changes in moral valuation: first, a difference in the notions of "bad" and "evil," and second, different interpretations of "good" juxtaposed to these two notions (Nietzsche [1887] 1967, 40). Concerning the former, the qualities that the nobles had considered as "bad," the slaves now labeled as "good," and they associated "evil" with the characteristics of their oppressors. As to the latter, the noble person's notion of good was derived "in advance and spontaneously out of him" (39). It was the noble person's original affirmation and perception of him- or herself. The dominant (inverted) notion of good, however, rose out of the context of the slave, evolving out of the slave's resentment in response to the nobles. In other words, as Nietzsche says, "an afterthought" (39).

Nietzsche asserts that there is something inherently religious in slave morality. He believes slave morality needs a god, a transcendent all-powerful being, to furnish substance to the poor in return for their virtues, humility, and meekness. The inversion of moral values ensures that the poor will have a good life—if not in this life, then certainly in the next. These moral values become systematized metaphysically in Christianity, which Nietzsche calls the "poison [that runs] through the entire body of mankind" (Nietzsche [1887] 1967, 36).

Christianity claims that although there is not justice in this world, there is another world where God's justice reigns eternal. Christianity also asserts that everyone gets what he or she deserves in the afterlife. Nietzsche says this belief rises out of the impotence and anger of slaves in the physical realm and was transformed into a myth where the slaves get revenge on the oppressor—if not in this world, at least in the next (Nietzsche [1887] 1967). Nietzsche argues that the slaves are weak. The Romans, on the other hand, are the strong, fierce, independent, warlike men. Although he admits that "Rome has been defeated" (53), according to Nietzsche, the Romans showed no reluctance to inflict pain upon inferior peoples. The Romans were guided by natural drives and instinct. Therefore, Nietzsche ([1887] 1967) wishes to supplant slave morality with a new type of noble morality. He opposes the values of the weak, those rising out of the instinct of *ressentiment* (or resentment), having such dominance in society. He hopes to ignite a counterrevolution, one in which the stronger, warlike values of the ancient world will reign.

Thus, Nietzsche ([1887] 1967) wants to go "beyond good and evil," slave morality and Christian morals. He thinks these belief systems are based on pity and inferiority and have deep associations with the weak. Nietzsche wants to move toward a new master morality, a potent, capable morality where judgments are based on strength and where the highest type of human being is realized. Nietzsche envisages that master morality will produce *sovereign individuals* who are "autonomous and supramoral." The sovereign person is proud of "the extraordinary privilege of *responsibility*" (59), the consciousness of freedom, and the power over him- or herself and his or her own fate. The sovereign person feels life and strives for ever-greater expressions of power. However, such power is not simply defined as having power over others; it is also the discharge of instinct throughout the world. Thus, this person of master morality accomplishes great things; he or she despises mere mediocrity and acts out of a "dominating instinct" (60). The sovereign person, says Nietzsche, calls this dominating instinct *conscience*.

Nietzsche nevertheless recognizes value in slave morality. It makes humans better than animals, he says. Nietzsche calls this paradoxical aspect of slave morality "bad conscience" ([1887] 1967, 62), and he regards it as an illness whose future brings forth guilt (85). Guilt provides humans with a depth that they would otherwise lack. It creates in them a soul – a soul that yearns to be free. Humans thus become self-conscious beings capable of being divided against themselves. Self-consciousness, however, also fosters an ongoing self-relationship based on an attitude of hatred toward one's own instinct. Thus, Nietzsche wants to reject the valuations of good and evil but not necessarily all of slave morality. Guilt, however, is necessary for morality, particularly where actions occur out of duty rather than for external reasons like punishment. In other words, guilt has value because it causes humans to go through a period of alienation on their way to becoming self-governed and autonomous beings.

But how does guilt relate to Christianity? Nietzsche argues that guilt rises from the relationship between debt and punishment. Morality presupposes bad conscience that has its origin in the material idea of "debts" (Nietzsche [1887] 1967, 62–63). Although this type of guilt involves the feeling of indebtedness felt toward ancestors, God, or a neighbor, it primarily has to do with one's own nature. The idea of indebtedness, according to Nietzsche, is based in the contractual relationship between creditor and debtor (63). The punishment associated with debt is not necessarily the kind imposed for doing wrong; but is also not the kind that parents imposed on their children, "from anger at some harm or injury, vented on the one who caused it" (63). Nietzsche argues that the idea of punishment is a practice that leads us to understand ourselves as human beings and our instinct toward cruelty—an instinct exemplified in ancient times, when executions and torture were part of festive occasions and pleasure was gained by inflicting pain (65, 67).

"The man of *ressentiment*," asserts Nietzsche, "invented the 'bad conscience'" ([1887] 1967, 75) in response to memories and out of the conditions of social living. The state and the administration of law play a vital role in the way humans express resentment (74). The state has essentially taken "the object of *ressentiment* out of the hands of revenge," substituted "for revenge the struggle against the enemies of peace and order," devised and imposed settlements, and elevated "certain equivalents for injuries into norms to which from then on *ressentiment* is once and for all directed" (75). Thus, violence and capricious acts on the part of

> individuals or entire groups as offenses against the
> law, as rebellion against the supreme power itself,
> and thus leads the feelings of its subjects away

from the direct injury caused by such offenses.
(Nietzsche [1887] 1967, 76)

Civil society and the establishment of legal order suppress and
redirect instincts "as a means of *preventing* all struggle" (Nietzsche
[1887] 1967, 76). Although the restraint of natural instincts is
necessary for human survival and social well-being, civil society is
the ground that gives birth to and nurtures the bad conscience. The
natural instincts and animal drives that are innate to human beings
are suppressed within the walls of society. Instincts that would
otherwise discharge themselves outwardly instead inevitably turn
back on their human carriers, becoming internalized, along with
the accompanying cruelty and destruction. Nietzsche argues that
internalized punishment does not necessarily awaken "the *feeling of
guilt*" (81); however, it does destroy "vital energy and brings about
a miserable prostration and self-abasement" (81). Essentially, self
"punishment *tames* men" (83).

Thus, Nietzsche seeks a return to the morality of the master race
to unleash the *instinct for freedom* or the will to power ([1887]
1967). The master type does not "know guilt, responsibility, or
consideration" (87). He does not deny himself and admires all
natural instincts as an aspect of being human. Conversely, the slave
suffers from guilt and resentment that manifest as internalized
cruelty and self-degradation. According to Nietzsche, the slave gets
pleasure from the idea of self-denial and self-sacrifice, both central
themes of Christianity (88), which poses an obstacle to the return
of master morality.

Christianity links internalized cruelty with indebtedness to God,
contends Nietzsche ([1887] 1967), where man finds himself
irreparable and unworthy. The doctrine embodies the principle

of virtuous guilt, wherein punishment gets turned back on the debtor, who is blamed for his or her own suffering. Nietzsche wants to free humankind from the feeling of guilty indebtedness and the enactment of internalized punishment. He claims that the accompanying alienation and bondage prevent humans from experiencing the essence of life—a free will—the ultimate freedom. Yet, although guilt is irredeemable, Christianity posits that there is a God who relieves the debtor of the burden of guilt.

Nietzsche proposes a new system of values based on self-mastery,[33] a mastery over instinct aimed at superior performance, even at the expense of others. Self-mastery, for Nietzsche, is not about autonomy. In fact, he uses self-mastery instead of autonomy because self-mastery brings forth and gives birth to the highest manifestation of human beings ([1887] 1967, 59–60). Nietzsche seeks to supplant the slave morals of Christianity and aims to bring back the morals of the warrior elite, where judgments will be enforced independent of metaphysical constructs. He argues that Christianity was created to articulate the perspective of the slaves, the weak, and the inferior. Consequently, it justified the way slaves took revenge out on the master class—the oppressors. Retaliation meant good was overcoming evil. But, the triumph of Christianity inhibits genius and creates myths based on notions of weakness and guilt. Thus, Nietzsche's desire to move beyond good and evil.

In conclusion, Nietzsche, with his critique of slave morals of Christianity and reintroduction of master morality, sees himself as untangling oppressive from liberating elements of Christianity. He seeks to open our eyes and minds to our greatness – a feat that Christianity has not been able to do, according to Nietzsche. He intends to liberate humankind from the shackles of guilt, resentment, weakness, and misery by inciting a moral revolt. As a free thinker, he is willing to challenge the dominant tenets of Christianity. Nietzsche believes that the triumph of Christianity is stifling humankind and preventing humanity from realizing its genius.

Nietzsche holds that the conditions of social living give rise to struggle, abuse, revenge, violence, intimidation, and capricious acts. He asserts that the triumph of Christianity in society leaves those who encounter corrupt and abusive forces feeling vulnerable, weak, and conflicted, which spark feelings of resentment. The memories and regrets associated with loss, powerlessness, or being forsaken in a time of need can result in 'bad conscience' or mental turmoil.

Yet for Nietzsche, the Christian God is not the author of sin, but He does permit sin. God permits sin because sin instills feelings of guilty indebtedness in the soul of humanity and arouses a yearning to be free. For the indebted, the revelation of God's infinite perfection is the highest conceivable good and the ultimate end of all His works. Without sin and feelings of guilt and resentment, there would be no manifestation of God's forgiveness unshackling us from our burdens and no demonstration of His love for humanity. Were there no bitter misery, there could be no sweet, tender mercy shown by God and no revelation of His grace.

Book 2

DIMENSIONS OF GOD
AND THE SELF

6

The Self

BOOK 2 FEATURES ESSAYS on God and the self. A reading of Charles Taylor's *Sources of the Self* (1989) deepened my desire to understand the self. His seminal work takes readers on a journey through the development and historical and theoretical analyses of selfhood. I gained great appreciation for his ability to construct, deconstruct, and reconstruct the self, while weaving theological and philosophical strands of knowledge. Taylor's work offers details and insights on the complexity of what being a self is about.

While we lack empirical evidence of God and the self, the abstract constructs and their elusive natures have not prevented humans from formulating mental representations of them. This book examines dimensions of God and the self from the perspectives of five major philosophical thinkers in the modern West. My aim is to draw upon their works to gain insight on how we can come to understand ourselves today. Each major thinker is considered independently, yet linkages are made between them. Two seventeenth-century philosophers are featured: René Descartes and John Locke. The transition into the eighteenth century is made with David Hume, Immanuel Kant, and Friedrich Schleiermacher.

This five-part project reveals an evolution in the construction of the conception of the self, particularly as it relates to God (also known as Source, Life Force, Higher Power, etc.).

Starting with Descartes, the self and God are imagined as ideas derived from deductive reasoning, but within two centuries, the self and God are derived from experience and envisaged as active forces in the world. Each thinker in this book defines the self in a different manner and emphasizes unique qualities and properties when discussing and using the concept. There is great appreciation for the fluid nature of these concepts and the complexity of usage and understanding.

While both terms, *self* and *God*, are symbols of abstract notions, they are both constructs that we are keenly aware of for most of our lives—whether we believe they exist or not. And yet, while there are degrees of self-consciousness and God-consciousness that range from less to more advanced stages of awareness; we are, for the most part, conscious of these concepts—although we may lack an understanding of their sources and composition. The less-advanced stages of self-consciousness manifest when there is an awareness of basic physiological functions, such as hunger, thirst, discomfort, and pain. We gain insights about this level of consciousness through our examination of Descartes's thinking self, Locke's sensing self, and Schleiermacher's feeling self. The more advanced stages of self-consciousness manifest when there is awareness of one's self in relation to transcendental or metaphysical objects, such as God. Here, our exploration of Hume's perceiving self and Kant's transcending self provides insights.

The transcendental or metaphysical conception of God moves beyond the notions of God as the Creator of the heavens and earth,

God as protector, God as punisher, and God as the giver of life. The investigation moves to an analysis of more complex notions of God postulated by theologians and philosophers, such as Hume's God, who is merely a perception, and Kant's God, who is an inference from the moral law. This complex array of notions and different aspects of God and the self are the focus of this book.

The work examines the works and thoughts of René Descartes (1596–1650), John Locke (1632–1704), David Hume (1711–1776), Immanuel Kant (1724–1804), and Friedrich Schleiermacher (1768–1834). From their works, one hears the voices of future philosophers and theologians. The dialectic between nineteenth-century Feuerbach and twentieth-century Barth on the nature of God as reflection of human nature or as something that exists independent of human nature already can be heard. One also gains a glimpse of Jamesian pragmatism with Hume's discussion of a continuous series of discrete perceptions, and with Schleiermacher's notions of self-consciousness and activity. The men featured in this book helped lay the foundation for the articulation and construction of conceptions of God and the self well into the twenty-first century and beyond.

7

Context: The Seventeenth Century— The Philosophical Revolution

*T*HE REFORMATION AND THE subsequent tension between Catholics and Protestants sparked religious and political conflicts across Europe. Religious wars and rebellions raged from Spain to Sweden. Beginning with the 1524 peasant uprising in Germany, adherents of Catholicism and Protestantism lashed out at each other in efforts to gain control of provinces and territories. (Palmer & Colton 1995) Protestant advances aroused hostility among Catholic theologians, which resulted in the Counter-Reformation. In 1562, civil war began in France. The religious strife between Protestant Huguenots and Catholics finally ended with the Edict of Nantes (1589), legislating toleration of Protestants. (The edict would later be revoked in 1685.) Twenty-five years of war raged in Protestant Germany after the Hapsburgs sought restoration of Catholicism. With the Peace of Augsburg in 1555, religious authority was given to local lords to determine the religion of their subjects, however, such religious liberty would not fully be realized until the end of the Thirty Years' War (1618–48), with the Peace of Westphalia. During this thirty-year period, England, Sweden, France, Germany, Spain, and others fought. After decades of violence, the Europeans were weary and despondent. Germany, already devastated by the loss of population and poverty, was hit especially hard by famine, plunder, and pestilence. Because of the pain and suffering left by war, the notions of religious tolerance and pluralism became more attractive. (Palmer & Colton 1995)

It was also during this tumultuous period that science was taken into new and revolutionary directions. The Italian Galileo Galilei (1564–1642), who upheld Copernicus's notion of a sun-centered cosmos, further highlighted the Copernican theory by explaining the changes of light and shade on the moon in his *Starry Messenger* (1610). A century earlier, Nicolaus Copernicus (1473–1543) had completed *Concerning the Revolution of the Celestial Bodies*, challenging Aristotle's scheme that placed an immovable Earth at the center of the cosmos, with luminous heavenly bodies rotating around it. Copernicus contended that Earth was not set in a steady state and shifted it into the realm with the rotating heavenly bodies. Religious leaders, including Luther and Calvin, condemned his work. Copernicus's failure to show observational proofs of his claims served to strengthen the condemnation against him. (Taylor 1989; Palmer & Colton 1995)

Galileo's work intensified the intellectual debate around Copernicus. He also called into question Aristotle's cosmology of a fixed cosmos, which was compatible with the theology of the Catholic Church. Aristotle, and later Plato, believed that the universe was composed of individual particles moving according to the law of God in an orderly fashion. They therefore placed the sources of moral strength in the cosmos and held that human beings must look outside themselves for moral authority. "To have access to the higher," contended the ancient moralists, "is to be turned towards and in tune with this cosmic order, which is shaped by the Good" (Taylor 1989, 143). God was the force operating in the universe, and to know Him was to know the operations of the cosmic order.

The discoveries of Galileo are based on radical notions of empirical knowledge and new analytical theories that resulted in the formulation of advanced laws of the cosmos, structures of the universe, and the laws of gravity. These new scientific achievements created disorientation and the breakdown of traditional institutions and belief systems. The sun-centered cosmology of Galileo, which

> claimed that the earth was in motion appeared to conflict with some biblical passages which seemed to imply the stability of the earth. Most fundamental of all, in claiming to have established the truth of the sun-centered cosmology Galileo was in conflict with the Church's view of theology as the queen of the sciences, and of the claims of theology to have authority over all other forms of knowledge. (Harman 1983, 19)

The clash between Galileo and the Catholic Church was symbolic of the antagonism between scientific and religious authority. The Church fought to hold on to its supremacy by admonishing Galileo and condemning the works of Copernicus. Yet, the works of Copernicus, Galileo, and René Descartes would lead the way in profoundly influencing the Scientific Revolution.

In the seventeenth century, there were two major strands of anti-Aristotelian thought. The first, associated with Descartes, was known as Rationalism. This strand held that reason alone derives knowledge of truth about the world in which we live. This perspective also contended that senses and passions needed to be tamed because of their ability to deceive. The second strain, Empiricism, associated with John Locke, postulates that it is not the passions or senses that must be contained, but reason. This view contends that it is impossible to know the reality of things beyond experiences, and true knowledge is derived from the senses. In reality, the views of Descartes and Locke were not as starkly opposed as they appear. On some points, Descartes becomes an empiricist, while on other positions, Locke sounds like a rationalist.

8

Descartes's Thinking Self

$\mathcal{R}$ENÉ DESCARTES (1596–1650), PHILOSOPHER and mathematician, lived amid religious and scientific upheaval. Uncertainty was spreading as beliefs espoused by once-trusted authorities appeared to crumble, and nothing seemed certain as scientific and theological theories contradicted one another. Descartes's search for epistemological certainty began with his program of systematic doubting. Descartes began by adapting a mathematical method to philosophical thought. He had hoped that this rational approach would result in practical knowledge based on absolute certainty. (Taylor 1989)

Descartes, weary of war, sought solutions to the uncontrollable passions of greed, rage, and hatred that he witnessed during years of devastation and violence. He questioned the powers of external religious and monarchal authorities. He challenged notions of morality, especially those based on the warrior as heroic figure. He yearned to formulate a theory that would promote "gaining mastery of oneself, shifting the hegemony from the senses to reason" (Taylor 1989, 143). Descartes elaborated in saying that this "was a matter of changing the direction of our soul's vision…

To be ruled by reason was to be turned towards the Ideas" (Taylor 1989, 143). In essence, Descartes wants to internalize the warrior ethic and submit it to internal moral sources of authority.

Descartes underwent an experiment to see if he could eliminate all existing ideas, beliefs, traditions, and knowledge in order to obtain a clean mental slate. But first, he formulated a new method of attaining knowledge. Frustrated with the lack of certainty in most areas of study, he knew that traditional methods would not render the desired results. Descartes developed a methodology based on doubting and deductive reasoning that would ultimately lead to a new direction in science and philosophy.

Drawing upon his mechanistic worldview, which held that there are laws governing the natural order, Descartes concluded that there are only two sorts of substances: mental and physical. From this claim, he formulated his notion of mind-body dualism, where the mind is associated with the spiritual realm and the body with the material. He bifurcated the self into two distinct entities: spirit, which he characterized as thinking substance; and matter, characterized as material substance. This was a new conceptual framework for scientifically theorizing about the self.

Descartes argues that knowledge is comprised of a set of innate ideas, constructed in the mind that do not depend upon experience or any form of external authority. To eliminate or at least minimize the importance of external authority, Descartes transitioned the source of moral authority from outside the self in a fixed cosmos to inside the self, where ordering ideas through reason occurs. The separation of the human being into matter and spirit forms the foundation of Descartes's new philosophy. Humanity is no longer dependent upon a fixed cosmos to encounter God. In fact, Descartes's radical project shifts from "the imperfect self" and "perfect God" outside the self, to "an encounter with God within" the self (Taylor 1989, 157), to the realization that the existence of God is inseparable from the thinking self. A meeting with God is a meeting with a self-sufficient self. (Descartes 1993) His theory shatters the basis upon which the Church had justified its hierarchical authority. Each human being is now solely dependent upon him- or herself for dignity, self-esteem, encounters with God, and moral authority.

Descartes's scientific and philosophical theories transformed the basis upon which material and cognitive explanations were constructed. While Descartes's scientific thought would have a tremendous impact on the way objects, matter, and natural processes would be studied, his philosophical thought relating to ideas and thinking substances was equally radical.

Descartes's program of systematic doubting, outlined in his 1637 work *Discourse on Method*, aims to subject every idea to rigorous examination. Instead of seeking authority through external sources such as the Church, the Bible, the Holy Spirit, religious leaders, and political rulers, he turns inward as a means of finding a sound basis for knowledge. He looks for internal authority. (Taylor 1989) For Descartes, truth is marked by the attainment of clarity and certainty. He concludes from his experiment that knowledge cannot be reduced beyond the single idea of his own existence. The only notion he accepts absolutely is "I think, therefore I am" ([1637] 1993, 18-19).

While Descartes knows that he *himself* is true and certain, he admits to the arduous nature of examining and eliminating all ideas and traditions. He confesses that "a certain laziness brings me back to my customary way of living" (Descartes 1993, 63). No matter how disciplined Descartes becomes, he realizes his inability to eradicate all ideas and objects. Some ideas and objects, he admits, like the sky, trees, earth, God, the self, and other human beings, are out of his control. These objects exist independently of him. Yet, he contends that he continues to construct notions of them in his mind. His rationale goes like this: If the objects are true and certain, they are aspects of my own nature because I myself am true and certain. But if they are not true and certain, then I perceive defective ideas, and therefore I also have imperfections. This circular logic reveals an implicit paradox in Descartes's philosophical methodology. If we are comprised of a set of innate ideas that are constructed in the mind, then the notion *I think, therefore I am*—when taken to its full conclusion—also means *I think, therefore you are* and *I think, therefore it is*. But the objects about which I think also inform my thinking, and I project back on to them positive or negative attributes, not only that I assume about the objects but also the positive or negative qualities inside me, based on my disposition at the moment.

According to Descartes, we are what we think. Descartes knows that he exists because he thinks about objects. Nevertheless, he ponders: What does the thinking substance I called "I" actually consist of? Is my nature finite, like that of other material objects? Or is it infinite and eternal, like that of God? Perhaps, states Descartes, "I am something greater than I myself understand. Perhaps all these perfections that I am attributing to God are somehow in me potentially, although they do not yet assert themselves and are not yet actualized" ([1637] 1993, 78).

This reasoning reveals the paradoxical loop that alternates between certainty and uncertainty in Descartes's philosophy. While Descartes's subjective *I* or self is certain that *he thinks*, his identity is based upon the objects perceived and thought about. This reflexive process, in turn yields uncertainty because when objects are in motion, they change and transform over time. It is through relationships with objects that Descartes becomes profoundly aware of his own finitude and imperfection. Realizing this, he imagines that he is dependent upon a substance much greater and more perfect than himself. He rationalizes that this perfect, infinite being must exist because he can conceive Him in his mind. He then concludes that this perfect being must exist outside of him, because he is already aware of *his* own imperfections, and nothing perfect can reside inside of imperfection.

> I certainly could not obtain [the idea of a being more perfect than my own] from myself. It thus remained that this idea was placed in me by a nature truly more perfect than I was, and even that it had within itself all the perfections of which I could have any idea, that is, to put my case in a single word, that this nature was God. To this I added that, since I knew of some perfections that I did not possess, I was not the only being in existence… but that of necessity it must be the case that there is something else more perfect, upon which I depended, and from which I acquire all that I had. (Descartes [1637] 1993, 20)

While Descartes argues that human beings construct ideas and concepts in their minds, he posits that the perfect beings we conceive of are derived from sources we do not possess. Their existence lies outside our innate ideas. Descartes reflects,

> I must consider whether there is anything in this idea [God] that could not have originated from

me. I understand by the name "God" a certain substance that is infinite, independent, supremely intelligent and supremely powerful, and that created me long with everything else that exists— if anything else exists. ([1637] 1993, 76)

Aware of his own finitude and imperfections, Descartes reasons that there must be a God, an infinite, perfect being, or else he would not be able to conceptualize His being. Descartes reasons further that there is something eternal that has always existed. That something is God.

[T]he more carefully I focus my attention on them [the predicates of God], the less possible it seems they could have arisen from myself alone. Thus, from what has been said, I must conclude that God necessarily exists [because He is infinite and greater than I and more supreme and intelligent than I]. For although the idea of substance is in me by virtue of the fact that I am a substance, that fact is not sufficient to explain my having the idea of an infinite substance, since I am finite, unless this idea proceeded from some substance which really was infinite. Nor should I think that I do not perceive the infinite by means of a true idea, but only through a negation of the finite, just as I perceive rest and darkness by means of a negation of motion and light (Descartes [1637] 1993, 77).

It was upon this foundation that Descartes constructed the knowledge of God. Descartes admits that he is a created being brought to life by a Creator, and he posits that God's certainty can be attained only through an inward search of critical knowledge of self. He writes:

> When I turn the mind's eye toward myself, I understand not only that I am something incomplete and dependent upon another, something aspiring indefinitely for greater and greater or better things, but also that the being on whom I depend has in himself all those greater things—not merely indefinitely and potentially, but infinitely and actually, and thus that he is God. The whole force of the argument rests on the fact that I recognize that it would be impossible for me to exist, being of such a nature as I am (namely, having in me the idea of God), unless God did in fact exist. God, I say, that same being the idea of whom is in me: a being having all those perfections that I cannot comprehend, but can somehow touch with my thought, and being subject to no defects whatever. (Descartes [1637] 1993, 81)

First, Descartes deduces that there must be a Creator because he has played no part in his own creation. He looks around and sees other beings and objects that he has played no part in creating, and he assumes that they also have played no part in their own creation either. Secondly, Descartes concludes that this Creator must be more perfect than himself because the Creator has imparted the idea of a perfect being in his mind. He, therefore, can construct the idea of God because God is in him. God has caused him to exist and have knowledge of Him because he is in God. Thus, there are two things that Descartes knows for sure: that he exists, and that there is an infinite, perfect God.

Descartes's theory, writes Charles Taylor in *Sources of the Self: The Making of Modern Identity*, "gives Augustian inwardness a radical twist and takes it in a quite new direction" (1989, 143). His theory places emphasis on the importance of cognition and the transposition of the sources of moral authority from outside to inside. This approach discredits traditional claims of knowledge of God. Descartes proves that God is not found through external authority such as the church, the Bible, the sacraments, or any revelation based on an external search. All external authority is removed. Descartes's God and sources of authority are found through the natural power of imagination and rationalization in an inward fashion.

According to Descartes, self-knowledge is attained through the reflexive process of subject-object dualism. Self-awareness and consciousness of the limits of self are realized upon encounters with other objects. Descartes's dualistic process objectifies the self, and the *subjective I* respond to its *objective self,* just as it would respond to any other object encountered. This move creates an artificial division between the subjective and objective natures of the self. Ironically, Descartes's project to base knowledge of self on truth and certainty falls short. The objectification of the self essentially entraps the self in a circular loop of uncertainty because of the object-dependent nature of the *subjective I.*

Descartes had hoped to make the existence of self independent of matter and external objects. He theoretically formulates the dualistic nature of self by freeing the soul—or thinking self— from the body (matter); but practically, a bifurcation of the self is impossible, and the dualism never existed. The subject-object dependency essentially renders the division of "self" fiction. The self is constantly aware of its finite nature and imperfections because its *identity* is based on matter and external objects. The only way

Descartes can escape this enigma is by postulating the notion of a perfect, unchanging, infinite being. When the self encounters this Supreme Being, he encounters perfection, truth, and certainty. Thus, the reflexive process between subject and object, in which the attention of the *subjective* self is focused on an infinite being, yields self-knowledge based on the attributes of the higher being.

Descartes's project, however, is riddled with tension and conflict. The paradox lies in the fact that Descartes seeks epistemological certainty through a subversive methodology based on doubting and uncertainty. He had hoped that this rational approach would result in practical knowledge based on absolute certainty. He seeks knowledge based on a circular process that requires positing the notion of God, a theoretical *idea* derived through deductive reasoning. Yet, our knowledge of God is dependent upon our knowledge of self. We come to know ourselves and God through a reflexive process; our perception of "God" is constructed from a combination of ideas or the negation and limitation of ideas based on objects encountered and experienced. We derive knowledge of ourselves and God through inquiry into reality. "To know reality is to have a correct representation of things—a correct picture within of outer reality, as it [comes] to be conceived" (Descartes [1637] 1993, 144). Descartes further declares "I [am certain that I] can have no knowledge of what is outside me expect by means of the ideas I have within me." Thus, we engage in theology only by means of critical knowledge of ourselves.

Problematic areas in Descartes's philosophy leave him open to criticism. Such critiques include, his methodology of doubt is merely a method of manufactured doubt and the fact that he fails to scrutinize ideas, such as the self, spirit, matter, and God. Yet, the achievements of his philosophical thought are substantial. In applying his method of skepticism to political, social, religious, and economic ideas, Descartes breaks theology's hold on philosophy. With philosophy autonomous and freed from external authority, he elevates it above theology. His project, even with its shortcomings, subverts the church, the Holy Spirit, and the Bible, and makes the notion of God dependent upon human reason and the imagination, while basing knowledge of self upon human experience.

Ancient mysticism and the theologies of Augustine, Luther, and Calvin provide the backdrop for the Cartesian philosophical-theological shift. Like Descartes's theology, these theologies elevate religious individualism (in varying degrees) and emphasize a direct relationship with God. Yet, each makes claims very different from those of Descartes. For instance, mysticism stresses a rejection of the world. But Descartes, while separating the self from worldly experience, does not reject the world. He sets the self apart from the world while remaining dependent on worldly objects and matter for self-knowledge. Augustine retains the Platonic notion that the order of things is based on a notion of the fixed cosmos, while Descartes shifts the fixed entity from the cosmos to the self. He then moves to construct the order of innate ideas by organizing them in the mind. The self is now the fixed, certain entity around which objects evolve. Luther maintains the importance of hierarchical ecclesiastical structures and a limited number of sacraments as necessary to access God, while Descartes totally rejects ecclesiastical structures and the sacraments as necessary to access God. Reasoning alone yields knowledge of God for Descartes. Calvin underscores the moral authority of the Bible and ecclesiastical structures as a precondition of knowledge of God, while Descartes, who is informed by Calvinistic doubting, eliminates all external sources of moral authority and internalizes them within. Human reason alone can establish God's existence. This claim not only challenges all prior claims that maintained that God imparts reason to human, it also discredits external authorities, dogmas, rituals, and inspired revelations as pathways to the Supreme Being.

In addition, Descartes's theological shift goes further than Luther or Calvin in the affirmation of ordinary life. In dignifying the certainty of self, one's relationship with God affords affirmation of any station in life. As a result of cognition and internalized reasoning, one's moral worth is now found in the self. A thinking substance can know God personally without external interference or domination. Such a theological shift is necessary, believes Descartes, if the religious wars of his times are to end. Writes Taylor of Descartes's philosophical aim, his

> ethic of rational control, finding its sources in a sense of dignity and self-esteem, transposes *inward* something of the spirit of the honour ethic. No longer are we winning fame in public spaces; we act to maintain our sense of worth in our own eyes. (1989, 152)

With Descartes, the modern man emerges. Ordinary life is further affirmed, and inner dignity and worth become more important than public fame through behaviors based on the warrior ethic. For Descartes, this shift is not only important for religious and political tolerance; it also is important for the inner peace of the individual. The internalization of moral authority, argues Descartes, would increase man's ability to control his rage, greed, and brutish nature.

While the passions of the body insured man's survival, they needed to be tamed through reason of the mind. "Descartes offers a new understanding of reason, and hence of its hegemony over the passions" (Taylor 1989, 144).

While Descartes's methodological skepticism results in an artificial division of the body and mind, this philosophical claim gives rise to the modern notion of the self, one who is self-defined through a reflexive subject-object process. It is through the process of subjective disengagement that Descartes finds certainty and self-confidence in his own, and consequently, God's existence; but the presence of doubt regarding all else leads Descartes to continue his search for certainty in order to control and stabilize the self. To attain better knowledge to predict and control the self, Descartes's thinking self finds it necessary to observe and measure the structure and movement of objects outside himself.

It is important to emphasize one last point about the contradictory nature of the existential claims in Descartes's philosophical theory before moving on to the discussion of Locke's notions of God and self. On the one hand, Descartes's assertions claim to set the individual mind (or soul) free; on the other hand, they justify further the domination and exploitation of others—things, animals, individuals, peoples, or places, thus depriving them of their normative force in the world once objectified. The control and manipulation of objects are inevitable when individuals seek to reduce the uncertainty and instability associated with their own identities and existence. Essentially, Descartes further legitimizes the domination and control of things classified as objects by the more powerful in society. Moral, political, and social insecurities result from uncertainty. To increase stability and feel more secure, it becomes necessary for human beings to control and monitor others. Cartesian philosophy, therefore, justifies an atomistic view of life, where a collective of self-serving individuals can contribute further to the misery and oppression of others in society.

9

Locke's Sensing Self

$\mathcal{C}$ARTESIAN PHILOSOPHY INTRIGUED JOHN Locke (1632–1704), who familiarized himself with Descartes's work while in Paris between 1674 and 1679. While Locke embraced some aspects of Cartesian philosophy, like anti-Aristotelianism and mind-body dualism, he disagreed with several of its theoretical claims. Descartes had been concerned about the distortion of truth claims and their consequent deception. His philosophical project sought analytical methods that would derive knowledge based on certainty and truth. Descartes wanted each individual to recognize his or her own ability to reason and formulate beliefs and opinions without external interference. (Taylor 1989) Locke, on the other hand, formulates a notion of self that seeks useful knowledge based on experience in the world. Locke

> aligns himself against any view which sees us as naturally tending to or attuned to the truth, whether it be of the ancient variety, that we are qua rational beings constitutionally disposed to recognize the rational order of things; or of the modern variety, that we have innate ideas, or an

innate tendency to unfold our thought towards the
truth. (Taylor 1989, 165)

Locke disagrees with Descartes's claim that ideas are innate; Locke
does not believe that we are born with ideas implanted by God.
For him, it is our mental faculties that are innate, the capacities to
perceive and process ideas for understanding. Locke argues that
all ideas are derived from experience of the world. Knowledge
is ascertained only through acquired ideas that arise from sense
experience. Locke asserts that we are unable to know the reality
of things beyond our experiences of them. He contends that the
mind is a *tabula rasa*, a blank slate upon which ideas are transcribed
based on experience. For Locke, this argument supports his claim
that knowledge is always open to correction by further experience.
He maintains that there are limits to human knowledge given
that knowledge is unattainable beyond human experience; yet,
certainty is impossible because the next set of experiences always
threatens to revise truth claims. In other words, the notion of
self and our understanding of ourselves are constantly evolving.
For this reason, Locke believes true knowledge is distorted and
hindered by tradition, language, and mysteries (Taylor 1989, 165),
which seek unsuccessfully to concretize beliefs, knowledge, and
opinions. Properly formulated beliefs, knowledge, and opinions—
those based on experience—would rectify problems of deception.

As a young man, Locke grew up in the midst of revolutionary change
in the religious and political life of England. He witnessed the
English Civil War (1642), when Parliament and the king engaged in
open warfare over whether Anglicanism or Presbyterianism would
be established in the kingdom. He was a young man when Charles
I was put to death and the Interregnum and Commonwealth
were declared (1649). In that same year, religious toleration was

decreed for all except Unitarians, atheists, Roman Catholics, and some Anglicans. He was twenty-eight years old at the time of the monarchical Restoration in 1660, when Charles II, who was inclined toward Catholicism, became king. The Church of England and the Parliament were also restored during this time. (Palmer & Colton 1995)

Shortly after the Restoration, the king and Parliament were at odds once again. When the king died in 1685, his brother James II assumed the throne. James was a more devout Catholic than his brother, Charles. His policies threatened the Anglican monopoly of church and state. With pressures mounting from opposition and the invasion of England by the Dutchman William of Orange at hand, James fled to France. While Louis XIV sought to restore the Catholic dynasty in England, the English fought against it. They knew that restoration of the Stuart dynasty would mean royal absolutism. In 1688, the year of the Glorious Revolution, Protestants William of Orange and his wife Mary were proclaimed corulers of England (Locke [1689] 1975, xiv). In 1689, Parliament enacted legislation upholding the rights of citizens. They included enactments preventing the suspension of a law by the king, allowing Protestants to practice their religion. They also put an end to arrest and detainment without legal process. Also during this year, Locke published his *An Essay Concerning Human Understanding*. (Palmer & Colton 1995)

Locke supported Parliament's stance against absolutism. He also felt that the Glorious Revolution was justified; but during these turbulent decades when Catholics, Anglicans, and Protestants sought sole control of church and state, Locke was deeply disturbed by the miserable condition of the populace. He strongly believed in the dignity of man and contended that natural rights were inherent to all people. Locke believed that Cartesian philosophy had contributed to the minimization or total neglect of the natural rights that people possessed. While he considered himself a dualist, he took a stance at odds with Cartesian thought when it came to innate ideas. He believed that both people and physical objects possessed powers and natural properties based on material and spiritual essences. According to Locke, individuals, animals, and objects all have innate qualities and attributes that deserve respect.

By recognizing the dignity of people and things, he affirms and values both subject and object. Human beings—every individual self—and the objects they encounter are endowed with natural properties. Knowledge and our understanding of our selves are, therefore, derived from our experiences in the world with objects that possess innate qualities. This is the basis of the doctrine of Empiricism: there are no innate ideas. Ideas, including our notions of God and the self, are acquired from experience, and they inform and become our knowledge about the world around us.

Locke believed that it was his calling to transform philosophical thought. "One permanently formative part of his upbringing was his induction into his parents' determined Protestant faith," writes Peter H. Nidditch in the introduction to Locke's *Essay* ([1689] 1975, x). As a result, Locke moves aggressively into the philosophical task ahead of him, "stress[ing] the vital role of the search and application of experienced fact in the accumulation and testing of truth" (xvii). He believes God will guide and sustain him in this "crucial first task ... of demolition, and Locke speaks of his ambition as 'to be employed as an under-labourer in clearing the ground a little, and removing some of the rubbish that lies in the way to knowledge'" (Taylor 1989, 165–6). The second crucial task for Locke was rebuilding knowledge "out of the building blocks of simple ideas" for practical use. (166)

There are two sources of experience from which knowledge is derived, according to Locke. The first source by which ideas are formed in the mind is *sensation*. The second is *reflection*. Sensations are experienced when the things of the world strike one or more of the five senses, consequently transmitting messages to the mind. Sensations result from distinct perceptions such as the awareness of the heat of fire, the sight of the blue color of the sky, the sweet taste of sugar, the sound of a soft purr of a kitten, or the spoiled smell of sour milk. Reflections are experienced after ideas are stored in the mind and our mental operations utilize them for *"Perception, Thinking, Doubting, Believing, Reasoning, Knowing, Willing,* and all the different actings of our own Minds" (Locke [1689] 1975, 105). In essence, reflection is the "Mind ... reflecting on its own Operations within itself" and affording us ideas about what it is that our minds actually do.

Sensation and reflection are the sources of all human knowledge. To better understand the formulation of knowledge, Locke segments ideas into two categories: *simple* and *complex* ([1689] 1975, 119). Simple ideas are uncompounded and contain "nothing but *one uniform Appearance,* or Conception in the mind, and is not distinguishable into different *Ideas*" (119). A simple idea is transmitted to the mind as a result of one of the five senses, for instance, the dark rich color of coffee or its robust aroma. Simple ideas, however, can be combined and perceived in the same object, such as seeing, smelling, and tasting a cup of espresso. "Combining several simple *Ideas* into one compound one" (163) makes a complex idea, according to Locke, who offers a man and the universe as other examples. Yet, the mind "considered each [*complex Idea*] by itself, as one entire thing, and signified by one name" (164). Complex ideas can be decompounded and recompounded by the mind into endless varieties of ideas.

Cartesian philosophy moves to elevate the mind at the expense of the body, with the mind becoming the defining element of a human being. Locke, while agreeing with Cartesian mind-body dualism, disagrees with the mind being the primary defining characteristic of the human being. He maintains the distinction between the mind and body, while bringing them together as two atoms in a molecule. Though separate and distinct, they are bound together in union. Locke then moves to emphasize and prioritize sensing, recognizing that sense experience informs a thinking mind. It is the cognitive processes of finite spirits that allows them to know that they are physical beings occupying different spatiotemporal locations over time. According to Locke,

> the real self is ... nowhere but in this power to fix things as objects. This power reposes in consciousness. And thus Locke ... refuses to identify the self or person with any substance, material or immaterial, but makes it depend on consciousness. (Taylor 1989, 172)

Sensation provides the basis for all mental content, which results from the interplay of three determinants: the mind (the cognitive process of the subjective self), the object (mass, particles, or physical material that captures the attention of the self), and the percepts (the faded images of objects or sensory impressions transmitted to the mind). These three factors are foundational to Locke's theory of knowledge. This schema is also a major reason for the differentiation between the philosophical claims of Locke and Descartes. Locke proposes a

> new, unprecedentedly radical form of self-objectification. The disengagement both from the activities of thought and from our reflecting desires and taste allows us to see ourselves as objects of far-reaching reformation. Rational control can extend to the re-creation of our habits, and hence of ourselves. (Taylor 1989, 171)

According to Taylor, in his book *Sources of the Self: The Making of the Modern Identity*, Locke's disengaged self in theory destroys itself in order to properly and completely dislodge itself from its first-person status. Everything is objectified—even the self. All habits, beliefs, customs, and traditions are demolished to reconstruct a new self, so that the self that is engaged in the disengagement process can properly use mental capacities and functions for the reestablishment of new habits, beliefs, customs, and traditions to attain true knowledge. Essentially, Locke is calling us to engage in a process of "self-remaking" (Taylor 1989, 171). Taking care of ourselves, according to Locke, requires us to disengage in order to destroy our old selves. We become enlightened beings after using correct procedures and methods of rationality to reconstruct and reassemble ourselves, shaping our own character, reality, and view of the world. This is self-responsibility.

> [T]he modern ideal of disengagement requires a reflexive stance. We have to turn inward and become aware of our own activity and of the processes which form us. We have to take charge of constructing our own representation of the

world, which otherwise goes on without order
and consequently without science; we have to
take charge of the processes by which associations
form and shape our character and outlook.
Disengagement demands that we stop simply
living in the body or within our traditions or
habits and, by making them objects for us, subject
them to radical scrutiny and remaking ... Modern
disengagement by contrast calls us to a separation
from ourselves through self-objectification ... It
calls on me to be aware of *my* activity of thinking
or *my* processes of habituation, so as to disengage
from them and objectify them. (Taylor 1989,
174-5)

Locke acknowledges the possibility of distortion and uncertainty
in the reception of ideas and images by the mind. He admits
that truth and certainty, in terms of how ideas are perceived, are
not his ultimate objectives. He asserts that there is no certainty
of knowledge—all knowledge is subject to revision according
to a *person's* experience. His primary aim is not to establish the
certainty or truth of ideas and claims. Locke seeks to embark on
an in-depth examination of human understanding and identify
the "*Bounds* between Opinion and Knowledge" (Locke 1975, 44)
in order to improve the operations of the mind, develop correct
procedures for demolishing old knowledge and reconstructing
new knowledge, and ensure the possibility for proper practical
application of knowledge.

Locke wants human beings to become more adept at acquiring
and utilizing knowledge. He hopes that information about the
functioning of mental processes will lead to improvements in the

ability to reason and use other mental capacities. Locke believes that mental faculties are divinely imparted to help us make sense of the world, facilitate human survival, and improve ourselves and the world in which we live. His aim is to make knowledge practical in order to help humanity become more industrious and rational. "The first requires us to work hard, the second to be efficacious, to bring about 'Improvement'" (Taylor 1989, 238). Like Descartes, who sought to alter behavior by controlling greed, rage, and hatred, Locke seeks to enhance human productivity by eliminating slothfulness, covetousness, and ambition (240).

> In making our preservation the central point of God's will for us, Locke is following the Protestant affirmation of ordinary life ... God wants us to be productive, and this means that we should give ourselves energetically and intelligently to some useful task. Locke integrates into his own thought something like the Puritan notion of the calling ... The fact that God calls us to our particular line of work gives this a higher significance for us, but this entails a duty on our part to work hard at it and also as effectively as possible. (Taylor 1989, 238)

God's call to everyday types of work affirms ordinary life. Locke, like Descartes, inverts the values of traditional belief systems and hierarchical institutions. As more people come to believe that God favors their ordinary lives and are confident that such a life is worth living in order to please God, what had been

> a matter of living *worshipfully* for God, [becomes] a question of living *rationally* ... It is still[, however,] a question of following God's will, but this is now

understood in terms of rationality. Rising from
passion, blind prejudice, and unthinking custom
to reason confers the two related transformations:
it gives our own productive life order and dignity,
and it releases us from egoism and destructiveness
to benefit others. (Taylor 1989, 242)

Locke implies that there is a latent sense of God's presence in every
human life and that God is working in history as we use our mental
faculties to serve Him. Each human being has the seed of divinity
embedded within him- or herself—in his or her consciousness.
God has adapted our cognitive processes, not only to ensure our
survival but also that we might thrive and be "successful" in the
natural world.

According to Locke, God is one of three substances of which
human beings can have *ideas*. He writes of God's identity: "God
is without beginning, eternal, unalterable, and everywhere;
and therefore concerning his Identity, there can be no doubt"
(Locke [1689] 1975, 329). The other two are finite intelligences and
bodies. Finite intelligences have their solely designated time and
space to exist; and physical bodies are the same in spatiotemporal
location, as long as there is no addition or subtraction of matter.
Human beings, or finite intelligences, come to know God through
the *"intuitive Knowledge of [their] own Existence"* (618). From
experience, we become aware of the finite status of material
substance. We then reason that something causes finite material
to exist, because everything that exists has a cause. Since the
beginning of time, something has always caused objects to come
into being. Therefore, there must have always been a Creator. God
is that *something* that has existed since eternity and has caused all

material and spiritual substance to exist. God has always existed; He is infinite.

Locke's notion of God is similar to that of Descartes. They both arrive at the existence of God through deductive reasoning. From the perspective of finite human beings, they logically conclude that God is that *something* that has always existed and has brought us into existence. Locke declares "we are capable of *knowing*, i.e., *being certain that there is a* GOD, and how we may come by this certainty, I think we need go no farther than ourselves, and that undoubted Knowledge we have of our own Existence" ([1689] 1975, 619).

The self becomes the common denominator, in a continuous series of encounters with objects, in a world constantly in flux. According to Locke, *person* is the name for self (Locke [1689] 1975, 346), which is "a thinking intelligent Being, that has reason and reflection, and can consider itself as itself, the same thinking thing in different times and places" (335). Since Locke atomizes sense experience into a series of fragmented sensations (simple and complex), he recognizes the need to postulate continuity in life and moves to formulate the self as a unifying force that links all discrete sensations experienced in one life together in continuum. The self is that complex idea which helps to order and stabilize a person's life and environment. "When we see, hear, smell, taste, feel, meditate, or will anything, we know that we do so. Thus it is always as to our present Sensations and Perceptions: And by this everyone is to himself, that which he calls self" (335). Every self is therefore able to determine him- or herself from other selves and objects.

The self is that same conscious thinking thing with one life: it knows itself in the present, is aware of a past, and is able to connect a stream of thoughts into one continuous life that it only has experienced and continues to *feel*.

> Self ... (whatever Substance, made up of whether Spiritual, or Material, Simple, or Compounded, it matters not) ... is sensible, or conscious of Pleasure and Pain, capable of Happiness or Misery, and so is concern'd for itself, as far as that consciousness extends. (Locke [1689] 1975, 341)

While consciousness unites remote and present experiences into the same person, the absence of consciousness means that the substance is no longer itself (Locke [1689] 1975, 344–5).

Locke embraces a "notion of reason [that is] free from established custom and locally dominant authority" (Taylor 1989, 167). After severing thinking from passions, custom, and authority, Locke maintains that the proper use of reason yields independence and self-responsibility. Like Descartes, Locke challenges us to think for ourselves. He insists that "knowledge ... isn't genuine unless you develop it yourself" (167). For Locke, thinking for oneself makes one free. Locke equates cognitive freedom to self-mastery. Taylor writes: "And [this] is why Locke will speak often of the issue of reason in terms of the dramatic opposition of slavery and freedom. Freedom is difficult; it is hard to strike out on one's own, following one's own process of thought" (169).

The concept of self-mastery is crucial in Locke's philosophical thought. The notion also is central to Cartesian philosophy. Yet, both Locke and Descartes formulate differently the idea of self-mastery. Descartes conceives of the internal manifestation of self-mastery as the inward subsumption of the passions under the sovereignty of reason. The internal manifestation of self-mastery fosters a sense of moral dignity and self-esteem based on internalized personal worth, which is seen as the substitution for publicly recognized fame that is based on the warrior ethic and hero worship.

For Locke, self-mastery demands self-responsibility for one's own knowledge. Self-mastery requires the objectification of everything, including the self, and the process of disengagement. In order to be able to evaluate and take control of the self as a disengaged being, the self must have the courage to relinquish its first-person status in order to demolish all externally acquired customs, language, and traditions. Self-mastery is achieved by that individual who "can take this kind of radical stance of disengagement to himself or herself with a view to remaking" (Taylor 1989, 171) his or her self. Proper rebuilding, based on new and real knowledge, occurs only after one reassembles and reconstructs one's belief systems using one's own rational methods. Once this is achieved, the acquisition of self-knowledge continues to be gained through one's own experience and reasoning. This knowledge is then translated into industrious or rational action, which further informs one's experience.

Locke's philosophical thought plays a major role in setting the stage for eighteenth-century Deism, which bases the existence of God on reason and nature and not on supernatural revelation. His notion of the dignity and affirmation of all beings contributes to the deistic belief that there is a universal human nature. A second Lockean concept that contributes to the birth of Deism is the belief that knowledge is unattainable beyond experience. Deism seeks to eradicate miracles, mysteries, and superstition from true religion. It contends that there is a God, but humans do not have the capacity to know Him. God is only known through the systems of nature

He has created. A third Lockean notion is that of self-responsibility. Deism presupposes that the self-responsible autonomous individual with whom God relates to is a rational being. We are now in position to analyze eighteenth-century conceptions of God and the self.

10

Context: The Eighteenth Century— The Age of Empiricism

SEVENTEENTH-CENTURY DEBATES ABOUT THE existence and nature of God helped foster the environment that gave birth to Deism. With its claims for tolerance, equal access to God, and universal truths, Deism quickly gained a hold on contemporary thought. Intellectual wrangling over religious questions prompted a longing for religious peace, and deists were at the forefront of the movement to make peace a reality. In their effort to create an environment where ultimate truth could be ascertained, some deists concluded that all religions pointed to the same god. They also believed in one ubiquitous human nature and one true natural religion that formed the basis for all religions. Such beliefs are evident in the work *Christianity Not Mysterious* (1696) by John Toland (1670–1722), who seeks to eliminate mystery from revelation, remove the contradiction between reason and revelation, and elevate revelation to a form of knowledge parallel to reason. Toland contends that revelation, like reason, is accessible to everyone and is merely the result of truths derived from knowledge that lies beyond experience. Another deist, Matthew Tindal (1655–1733) maintains in his *Christianity as Old as Creation* (1730) that God and all His creation are perfect, and God deals with all men and knowledge equally and consistently. God, therefore, makes all truths accessible to everyone in the same manner. Tindal holds that religion is based on moral action and that everyone is able to recognize God's purpose for humankind.

Deism's appeal to subjectivity was a subtle assault on orthodox religion; "its aim ... to banish mysteries, miracles, and secrets from religion and to expose religion to the light of knowledge" (Cassirer 1951, 171) was viewed as an all-out attack on religious traditionalists. All deists, however, were not alike. In addition to the views of deists like Toland and Tindal, others "rejected altogether the need for revelation and faith," while others sought to prove that Christianity is "a wholly rational religion" (Hume [1779] 1990, 7). While many deists were strong advocates of toleration, their attacks on orthodox religion were considered forms of intolerance. These deistic claims fueled counterattacks, and David Hume was one of those poised to respond.

11

Hume's Perceiving Self

DAVID HUME (1711–1776) WAS born in Edinburgh into an affluent Scottish family. While he was reared in a devout Calvinist setting, he personally never found a need for religion. He received his education at the University of Edinburgh and was an avid writer on topics ranging from ethics and philosophy to history and political theory. During his life, he held several positions, some governmental in nature, and was also turned down at least twice for academic positions at universities because of his atheistic views. It would be *his* radical philosophical skepticism that would deal a fatal blow to the deist advance.

Hume's "opposition to deism is concerned neither with its doctrine of reason nor of revelation," writes Ernst Cassirer in *The Philosophy of the Enlightenment*. His objective is

> merely to evaluate [deism] from the viewpoint of the standards of experience, of pure factual knowledge … For the apparent 'human nature' on which deism proposed to base natural religion is itself no reality, but a mere fiction. Experience

reveals human nature to us in an entirely different
light from all the constructive attempts of the
deists ... The more penetrating our knowledge
of the nature of man and the more accurate our
description of this nature, the more it loses the
appearance of rationality and order. (1951, 178–9)

Hume sets out to undermine not only the fideistic claims of the
deists but also the theistic claims of the Christian rationalists and
adherents of natural theology.

At this point, it is first necessary to discuss Hume's epistemological
thought, which forms the basis for his conceptions of God and the self.
It is the springboard from which he launches his attack on religious
claims. Hume's epistemology divides mental representations into
impressions and ideas. Impressions are objects in the process of being
perceived, and ideas are perceptions distinguished by their lack of
vivacity and force. Impressions are determined by their veracity
(detail, precision, and sharpness) and ideas by their lack of clarity.
Since temporal relation influences mental representations, ideas
always follow impressions. Martin Bell, in his 1990 introduction to
Hume's *Dialogues Concerning Natural Religion*, writes:

Consciousness, for Hume, has two forms, feeling
and thinking. When we feel, the warmth of the fire,
the sensation of warmth, the sight of the flames,
and the pleasure we get are all perceptions of the
kind he calls "impressions." When we think, as
now, of such a situation, the perceptions before
our minds are called "ideas." Ideas, he argues, are
copies of and originate from impressions. (Hume
[1779] 1990, 12)

Hume maintains that the mind operates according to three principles: resemblance, contiguity, and cause and effect. *Resemblance* is the principle by which impressions or ideas appear similar. *Contiguity* is based on the temporal or spatial relations among objects, impressions, and ideas. *Cause and effect* is the principle based on the belief that a force gives rise to or results in the creation or movement of objects, impressions, or ideas. Everything we experience is said to have a cause, and we have become accustomed to the principle of causation because of the regularity of the sequential nature of events witnessed in life. Hume does not believe these principles correspond to any property in the world; he contends that they are instead properties of the mind.

Awareness of perceptions (i.e., impressions and ideas) is a presupposition for the recognition of one's self. The self emerges as the mind flows into a process of perceiving the continuous encounter with impressions and ideas. Hume's self is constantly in flux as it rapidly perceives discrete perceptions. His self is not a static, unified entity that *thinks* like the Cartesian self, but a perceiving, knowing self that is rapidly evolving in the process.

Hume, skeptical of the Cartesian self, therefore, sets out to destroy the notion of a divided being with his radical empiricist critique. He challenges the artificially construed relation of the subject "I" and object, and he argues that each person is a continuous stream of distinct perceptions. There is no "I" that holds the self in unison. According to Hume, the perceiver and perceptions are one and the same, there is no distinction between the two. In his *A Treatise of Human Nature*, he writes,

> when I enter most intimately into what I call *myself*,
> I always stumble on some particular perception or

other, of heat or cold, light or shade, love or hatred,
pain or pleasure. I never can catch *myself* at any
time without a perception, and never can observe
anything but the perception. ([1739] 1978, 252)

For Hume, there is no life without perceptions and no dualistic
nature in life. Human beings are merely a "collection of different
perceptions, which succeed each other with an inconceivable
rapidity, and are in a perpetual flux and movement ... They are
the successive perceptions only, that constitute the mind" (Hume
[1739] 1978, 252). Hume asserts that there is no firm foundation
to the "principle of individuation," the idea upon which the self and
God are based, because all objects vary and are interrupted. The
ease of transition between objects or perceptions tends to cause
erroneous acceptance of the notion of *sameness* of self, object, or
percept. There is no stable, constant impression or idea. There is
only the concept of diversity or multiplicity (201, 251–2), which is
the foundation for all conceptions.

Hume asserts that the common notion of *identity*, or sameness
of impression or idea, is absurd. We have a tendency to make the
mistake of equating *sameness* and *diversity* of impressions and ideas
because the physical and emotional changes in humans, objects,
and percepts are most often too gradual or incremental to alter
our image of them (Hume [1739] 1978). This error contributes
to the problems associated with the notion of identity because of
resembling objects and perceptions that, without reflection, *appear*
similar. These perceptions are variable and interrupted, yet they
are very easily connected and made whole by the mind, which
transmits an image of a continuous object (God) or person (self).
The confusion concerning identity is not based solely on the use of
the terms *sameness* and *diversity*. The problem is also that we have

come to believe a falsehood. By custom, we have come to live in error, and the propensity to accept fiction as reality is absurd to Hume.

> In order to justify to ourselves this absurdity, we often feign some new and unintelligible principle, that connects the objects together, and prevents their interruption or variation. Thus we feign the continued existence of the perceptions of our senses, to remove the interruption; and run into the notion of a *soul*, and *self*, and *substance*, to disguise the variation. (Hume [1739] 1978, 254)

Even the law of cause and effect, which appears to give unity and inner stability to our knowledge, is without foundation for Hume.

> [The law of cause and effect] is supported by no immediate evidence, and by no *a priori* significance and necessity; it is itself merely a product of the play of ideas which are connected to no objective, rational principles, but in their combination simply follow the workings of the imagination and obey its mechanical laws. And the same is true to an even greater degree of our religious ideas. (Cassirer 1951, 179)

Metaphysical concepts such as God, the self, and the soul, have no foundation in themselves. Even though they are derived from experience, they cannot be proven by experience. The principle of causation leads to the projection of empirically based ideas into the metaphysical realm, where memory and imagination are necessary for their continued existence. It is this process that gives rise to the metaphysical ideas Hume claims are erroneous.

The ideas and impressions that we perceive and reason about are derived from "what Hume calls the 'constant conjunction' of cause of effect," states Bell. (Hume [1779] 1990, 14). Constant conjunction is the mental process of action and reaction that is the product of prior experience with ideas and impressions. As a consequence of these previous experiences, we reason about causal relations that we do not perceive. Our experiences are therefore based on conjunctive relations, the process of an object, impression, or idea resulting from the actions of prior objects, impressions, or ideas. Although we can experience the objects that result from causal relations and witness a chain of events, we cannot witness the causal relation, the impetus of the effect or event, between objects, impressions, or ideas. Hume contends that experience is the basis for this type of reasoning. He calls it "probable reasoning" according to Bell, who further explains:

> We always make inferences which presume that causal connections in nature are *uniform*. Why? [Because we] ... infer it from the evidence of past experience. We would then be inferring it by probable reasoning. But ... it is circular to explain this by assuming probable reasoning already. (Hume [1779] 1990, 14)

The principle of cause and effect is fundamental to our knowledge of the physical world, and it allows for inferences between sense perception and metaphysical phenomena. Yet, causation cannot be known a priori. Our knowledge of cause and effect is the result of the experience of constant conjunction. "For Hume," writes Bell:

> what we do is to infer a cause or an effect ... from an effect or a cause that we currently experience.

> Our capacity to perform these causal inferences does not depend upon our having a scientific theory of how the cause produces the effect. In most cases we are simply ignorant of the inner workings of nature. (In fact, Hume believes that we never can have any *ultimate* explanation of why things happen in nature as they do.) (Hume [1779] 1990, 13)

For instance, the only way we know about the pull of gravity is by seeing an object fall once released. The constant conjunction is release-fall. Experience also reveals this knowledge in other causal relationships, such as knowing that fire burns. Hume, however, argues that relationships of constant conjunction are based on provisional truth. Our understanding of the earth's pull and fire's heat is always subject to revision as new experiences reveal new information. There may come a time when we release an object and it floats or when we are exposed to flames and not burned. Bell further explains:

> Hume's theoretical explanation of our beliefs about the causal properties of objects begins with his account of experience—it is from experience and not from *a priori* reflection that we discover that fire burns us ...; what gives Hume's account part of its distinctive character is his conception of experience. This conception has its origins in the thought of some of his predecessors, especially Descartes ..., [and] John Locke ... Experience is characterized subjectively, from the point of view of the person having the experience, and is a matter of the immediate content of consciousness.

> Our experience of fire, say, consists essentially in
> our having before our minds a *perception* of fire.
> ([1779] 1990, 11–12)

While our conceptions of God and the self are formulated as a consequence of the law of cause and effect, the law itself is supported by no empirical evidence and cannot be perceived. Therefore, according to Hume, the conceptions of God and the self result from the process of constant conjunction and cannot be proven in experience. They are not derived from an impression, and consequently there are no corresponding ideas for them. Hume writes: The self and God are not derived from "any one impression, but that to which our several impressions and ideas are supposed to have a reference" ([1739] 1978, 251). Hume contends that there are no external objects that can yield impressions such as self and God. We may come to experience the manifestations or effects of the self and God, but we are unable to point to the causal relation that creates these ideas. Hume asserts that we have come to assume the existence of the self and God through custom and faith—not experience.

Memory plays a vital function in the ability to hold perceptions in the mind, which is necessary to establish customs and traditions and engage in the practice of faith. Memory is operative in a stream of thought that flows through individual consciousness as well as intergenerational consciousness. Memory contributes to the facilitation of habits, as the mind becomes accustomed to expecting causal relations upon which *identity* and the independence of objects and percepts depend. Without memory, we would be unable to construct notions of God and self. The interactive function among experience, perception, causation, and memory is elemental in the construction of these notions.

As we reflect upon past and present experiences, the mind develops patterns through which impressions and ideas are channeled. These patterns facilitate mental activity and the formation of habitual actions in the mind. The development of mental habits is vital to human interaction and the emergence of the notions of God and self. In *The Enlightenment: The Rise of Modern Paganism*, Peter Gay writes:

> Hume argued, religion arose 'from a concern with regard to the events of life, and from the incessant hopes and fears, which actuate the human mind.' Confronted by a monstrous birth, the uncertainty of the seasons, by storms and a myriad of unexplained and seemingly inexplicable events, primitive man oriented himself in his world by inventing a large number of special, parochial deities: ... The anxious concern for happiness, the dread of future misery, the terror of death, the thirst of revenge, the appetite for food and other necessaries create hopes and, more significantly, arouse fears, and so 'men scrutinize, with a trembling curiosity, the course of future causes, and examine the various and contrary events of human life. And in this disordered scene, with eyes still more disordered and astonished, they see the first obscure traces of divinity'." (1966, 410–11)

Cassirer concurs and writes:

> appetites and passions are not only the source of the first religious ideas and dogmas; they are still the root of all religion ... It is the emotions of hope

and fear which have led men to adopt beliefs and which support their continuation in faith. Here we have the real foundation of religion. (1951, 179)

Cassirer further explains:

[Religion] arises from the fear of supernatural powers and from man's desire to propitiate these powers and subject them to his will. Here too it is the play of passion and of the imagination which controls and guides the currents of our religious life. Superstition and the fear of demons are the real roots of our conception of God. (1951, 180)

Hume holds that contemporary religious thought is a by-product of primitive constructs of deities and demons. (Gay 1966, 411)

Memory also plays a role in the intergenerational transfer and evolution of religious beliefs and ideas. Hume contends the "memory ... is to be considered ... as the source of ... identity" and maintains that "memory not only discovers the identity, but also contributes to its production, by producing the relation of resemblance among the perceptions. The case is the same whether we consider ourselves or others" (1978, 261). Additionally, he maintains that causal relation, memory, and imagination must be combined if we are to claim the notions of God and the self. Without causation, we have no present experiences. Without memory, we have no recollection of past impressions or ideas. Without imagination, we are unable to construct a continuous, unified object or percept, and there would be no identity of God or self.

Hume writes of imagination:

> the understanding never observes any real
> connection among objects ... when strictly
> examined, [it] resolves itself into a customary
> association of ideas ... [I]dentity is nothing really
> belonging to these different perceptions, and
> uniting them together; but is merely a quality,
> which we attribute to them, because of the union
> of their ideas in the imagination, when we reflect
> upon them ... It follows, that our notions of ...
> identity [of the self or God], proceed entirely from
> the smooth and uninterrupted progress of the
> thought along a train of connected ideas. ([1739]
> 1978, 259–60)

We can recall past ideas, though faded, of an object or a person
at different times, and with the imagination develop an idea that
incorporates drastic changes in appearance, disposition, and
presentation. We can alter old ideas stored in our memories and
through imagination adapt them to coincide with new impressions.
The mind has the capacity to integrate resemblances with
impressions through the imagination, to make an object appear
unified. Resemblances can also facilitate making objects appear
as a continued whole. Our notion of God's nature changes over
time, yet we hold the unified conception of God in mind. Our
appearance evolves over time, yet we continue to hold a notion
of a unified self. Hume asserts, "philosophy informs us, that
everything, which appears to the mind, is nothing but a perception"
(Bell 1990, 12), the self and God included. According to Hume, it
is the imagination that allows us to posit and believe the falsehood
of a unified self and God.

For Hume, the imagination is critical in the formation of what are perceived as stable images, formed from resembling impressions and ideas. These constant images are the result of combining disparate ideas that take on additional complexity when we ascribe to them an identity and independence. Causation, memory, and imagination are modes of thought that work together to help create illusions of a unified self-identity; yet, it is the principles of thought: resemblance, contiguity, and cause and effect that receive and associate impressions and ideas. But all are a posteriori principles informed by experience.

"Strictly speaking, we can have no *idea* of the [self or] divine nature," states Bell, who then quotes Hume: "Our ideas reach no farther than our experience. We have no experience of divine attributes and operations" (Hume [1779] 1990, 12). According to Hume, there is no such thing as an independent object with its own identity that exists outside the mind. Objects existing externally to my perceptions are an illusion.

It is this epistemological theory that Hume draws upon to counter the claims of Deism and natural religion. Hume resented the dogmatic nature of the religious. He contended that reason lacked the requisite power to prove claims of faith. According to Hume, the most holy religion is not perverted and can be attained by faith alone. He argues this point in his classic work *Dialogues Concerning Natural Religion*, which depicts a conversation among three characters each representing a different religious view: theism, deism, or skepticism.

Cleanthes, the theist, is the voice of Christian rationalism or natural theology. He maintains that God's existence can be determined a posteriori, from experience, and claims it is possible to prove the existence of God from matters of fact. He believes the human mind is similar in function to a more powerful divine intelligence and argues that by examining man-made objects, we can attain knowledge of God. This means that we infer from effects to learn about causes. The effects of human thought and wisdom are revealed in architectural masterpieces and precision watches (Hume [1779] 1990, 54–55). Cleanthes contends that it is through effects that we know the mind of the Author of nature resembles the human mind. "By this argument *a posteriori*, and by this argument alone, do we prove at once the existence of a Deity and his similarity to human mind and intelligence" (Hume [1779] 1990, 53), states Cleanthes.

Philo, the skeptic, who represents the views of Hume, questions the logic of any theory that attempts to find similarities between a building or a watch and nature or the universe. Philo wonders how a conclusion can be drawn from parts to the whole (Hume [1779] 1990, 58) and argues that humans are unable to grasp knowledge of the inner workings of the universe. He sardonically responds that perhaps the universe orders itself and there is no higher intelligence involved. Philo also charges theism with anthropomorphism, projecting human attributes onto the divinity. Doing so underestimates the significance of God and the universe. "What peculiar privilege has this little agitation of the brain which we call thought, that we must thus make it the model of the whole universe?" (58), asks Philo. This argument leads one to wonder whether humans create God in their image or whether God creates humans in His.

Nevertheless, Philo claims that it is erroneous to base the attributes of God on any aspect of human nature or what we see in nature. Philo contends that life is fraught with terror and anxiety resulting from the threats of both humanity and natural causes (Hume [1779] 1990, 105). Nature is no respecter of person when it comes to its wrath. He therefore questions how anyone could base their conception of the divine being on such unstable and potentially harmful forces. Hume holds that nature has no moral attributes, and to project qualities of good or evil upon nature or the causes of the universe is absurd. Hume believes there is an original cause, a God, whose motives and attributes are neither good nor bad. In other words, God and nature are neutral.

Demea, the deist and voice of fideism, seeks to prove the existence of God a priori. He is the mouthpiece of those who believe in a transcendent God that is beyond human comprehension. He claims that everything has a cause and assumes an infinite series of causes where the original cause "carries the *reason* of his existence in himself" (Hume [1779] 1990, 99). Yet, while we can infer a first cause, we are unable to comprehend its nature. For Demea, God's nature is a religious mystery. Deism contends that humans are

> Finite, weak, and blind creatures, we ought to humble ourselves in his august presence, and conscious of our frailties, adore in silence his infinite perfections which eye hath not seen, ear hath not heard, neither hath it entered into the heart of man to conceive. (Hume [1779] 1990, 51)

Since we are unable to comprehend God's nature, our understanding of Him is based on faith in His existence. Since ideas reach no further than experience, Philo expresses agreement with Demea and states: "it is a pleasure to me ... that just reasoning and sound piety here concur in the same conclusion, and both of them establish the adorably mysterious and incomprehensible nature of the supreme being" (Hume [1779] 1990, 53).

The a priori arguments of the deists and a posteriori of the theists both attempt to prove the existence of God. Ironically, Hume has never denied God's existence. The very fact that we conceive the *idea* of God presumes God's existence. To engage in deliberation to establish or deny the existence of God is to already have an *idea* of God in mind. Hume's questions center on the *nature* of God and whether it can be known. Deists degrade humanity as weak and feeble beings; because of human nature, humanity is incapable of knowing God, and it is impious and arrogant to even try. All we are able to do is sense the awesomeness of God. Demea holds "that each man feels, in a manner, the truth of religion within his own breast; and from a consciousness of his imbecility and misery, rather than from any reasoning, is led to seek protection from that being, on whom he and all nature is dependent" (Hume [1779] 1990, 103). The adherents of natural theology (as represented by Cleanthes) elevate humankind to ascertain knowledge of God by equating human intelligence with the mind of God. Cleanthes measures everything divine "by human rules and standards" (123). He believes that the human intellect is capable of grasping the nature and proving the existence of God.

Hume's radical skepticism leads him to posit that reason is incapable of proving the existence or nature of God. He also argues that even postulating the unity of a deity is erroneous. In the words of Philo, Hume states, "To be a philosophical sceptic is, in a man of letters, the first and most essential step towards being a sound, believing *Christian*" (Hume [1779] 1990, 139). Hume concludes that the postulation of God is based on faith alone. While at first glance this claim appears to support fideistic claims, ultimately it undermines

them. The circular logic of the skeptic proves subversive even to
the religious revelation of faith alone. The intellectual technique of
radical skepticism inevitably negates all claims, especially dogmatic
ones, and renders spurious any object external to our perceptions.
In the end, Hume's skeptical exercise leaves humanity mentally
fragmented, believing in nothing but one's own discrete ideas,
and abandoned without an existential foundation because all are
undermined—even faith.

12

Kant's Transcending Self

IMMANUEL KANT (1724–1804) WAS born in Prussia in 1724. Although social mobility was highly restricted in Prussia, its people remained hardworking and disciplined. Kant was raised in a pietistic setting, and his university studies centered on continental rationalism. His father was a saddler and his mother a devoutly religious woman who had hoped her son would one day become a pastor. Kant possessed a forceful inner drive and a radical, independent spirit that contributed to his belief that within each human being there is an unquenchable yearning for freedom. He opposed all forms of tyranny over the mind. Kant held that only free human beings could find God for themselves. The belief in the innate freedom of the human soul imbued Kant's philosophical thought.

Hume's writings had a profound effect upon Kant's thinking. He claimed that Hume had awakened him from a "dogmatic slumber" (Tarnas 1991, 341). Without rejecting Hume's fundamental insights into the principles of knowledge and modes of thought, Kant seeks to challenge Hume's skepticism and determinism. Hume had argued that all knowledge is subjective and empirically derived from continuous streams of impressions and ideas. Knowledge through reason is impossible, according to Hume. Only impressions and ideas in the mind yield knowledge. All external objects are illusions, posits Hume, and any assumed identity or independence is false.

Kant argues that Hume is deceptive in claiming the nonexistence of external objects. Unlike Hume, he contends that objects in the world are independent and have their own identities. They even exist when not being perceived. Yet, Staloff (1992) points out in a taped lecture that Kant maintains that it is impossible to know external objects as "things-in-themselves," objects in a state of pure, undistorted conception. Our perspectives influence all knowledge.

Hume's skepticism is considered subversive and threatens to render all external objects, truth claims, and metaphysical ideals erroneous, according to Kant. He believes Hume alienates the individual from the world and negates human interaction with objects and other human beings. Hume leaves the individual isolated, with perceptions alone. In addition, with the vast struggles for individual freedom going on across Europe, Kant feels Hume's determinism is counterproductive, jeopardizing all human freedom and leaving the human being, not only alienated, but also lacking self-determination and self-responsibility. (Sugrue 1992)

Kant wants to reconcile faith in God, freedom, and reason. He believes that rational beings acting in accordance with the moral law are free. Hume had called faith in God absurd, had sought to abolish freedom in determinism, and had rendered reason impotent in its ability to yield knowledge. Kant believes the only way to reconcile God, freedom, and reason, and counter skepticism and determinism, is with metaphysics. But to properly attack

Hume's philosophical claims, Kant must figure out how to obtain knowledge without depending on experience. Since experience is inherently selective and does not yield universal truths, Kant sets out to prove a priori knowledge is a possibility. In his 1781 classic *Critique of Pure Reason*, he contends that knowledge "prior to experience" yields universal, necessary truths. (Tarnas 1991; Staloff 1992)

Kant maintains that reason is a precondition of experience. Otherwise, he asserts, human beings would be unable to define and recognize objects, which exist even when not being perceived. Kant argues that knowledge is derived from the interdependence of experience and reason. Each offers necessary elements for the acquisition of knowledge—one provides "content," the other "form," and each constrains the other. The objective substance of experience constrains reason, and the mental forms, modes, and frameworks of thought constrain experience.

According to Kant, reason is an innate part of the mind. As a result of the mental frameworks given by nature, nature imparts a structure for making sense of mental operations, impressions, and ideas. That structure is reason. Experience is, therefore, necessary but insufficient for the acquisition of knowledge. We apprehend only the knowledge that reason allows us to.

In his *Critique of Pure Reason* (1781), Kant posits the existence of transcendental objects, those objects not subject to empirical investigation, such as God, the soul, and freedom. Since one's understanding of God does not come from sense experience, we cannot know God in this manner. Yet, we can know God outside experience. In order to prove this, Kant makes the distinction between the phenomenal and noumenal realms of the cosmos.

Objects of knowledge and experience are phenomena, while metaphysical objects are noumena.

Kant then delineates two aspects of the mind: (1) the empirical, ordinary, everyday consciousness that distinguishes its inner thoughts and feelings from the outer external world; and (2) the transcendental, a reflective mode of understanding objects that cannot be comprehended from sense data. Kant suggests "transcendental reflection" to solve the antinomy of metaphysical objects like God, the soul, and freedom. Transcendental reflection is necessary because it affords "each representation ... [a] place appointed in the corresponding faculty of cognition, and consequently the influence of the one faculty upon the other is made apparent" (Kant [1781] 1990, 188). Kant calls this reflective process the "transcendental dialectic," which illustrates how objects that go beyond the realm of phenomena exists in the realm of noumena. Kant writes:

> For we have here to do with a *natural* and unavoidable illusion, which rests upon subjective principles, and imposes these upon us as objective [principles] ... in imitation of the natural error. There is therefore a natural and unavoidable dialectic of pure reason ... which is an inseparable adjunct of human reason, and which, even after its illusion have been exposed, does not cease to deceive, and continually to lead reason into momentary errors, which it becomes necessary continually to remove. ([1781] 1990, 189)

Kant maintains that "theoretical cognition is *speculative* when it relates to an object or certain conceptions of an object which is not given and cannot be discovered by means of experience" ([1781] 1990, 355). Although God cannot be sufficiently proven through speculative reason (England 1968), the process reveals that the human mind has a natural disposition to apply the ideas transcendentally (Kant [1781] 1990). The transposition of objects produces metaphysical concepts.

Although the transcendental dialectic does not yield legitimate knowledge about the nature of God (Kant [1781] 1990), the transcendental idea, God, does have an important regulative function in our phenomenal inquiry and action. In his *Grounding for the Metaphysics of Morals* (1785), Kant illustrates a theoretical movement from speculative reason to a metaphysics of morals and outlines the practical nature that such ideas can have on human behavior in *Critique of Practical Reason* (1788).

Kant's moral philosophy presupposes self-consciousness. He defines the self as a being who recognizes that there is an "I" existing within him or her, or any person who is conscious of the subjective aspect of him- or herself in the world. Once the self recognizes its subjective nature, it is an agent originating its own actions. As the originator of its own actions, the agent considers itself free. Yet, Kant clarifies that this freedom is not achieved in the physical world of causal law but outside it. This freedom of self belongs to the transcendental (noumenal) realm. It is this "transcendental freedom" that belongs to Kant's rational agent. The concept of a free agent is the point of departure for Kant's moral theory.

Kant's notion of the self rises out of the Age of Enlightenment, a time when humanity claimed movement into maturity. With church authority circumscribed and nation-states emerging, there was a marked transition of more diverse groups of people moving into political, social, economic, and academic sectors. In addition to freedom being a political and social concept, Kant contends that it is also a moral one. Like the new scientific theories, political systems, and social structures that were emerging, Kant seeks to prove that a new kind of individual is also on the rise. This new individual or self is free, independent, and autonomous. The life of this new self is not predetermined, and its actions are not mechanical. The self is the master of its own destiny. Kant's moral philosophy centers on this new self-determined individual.

In the *Grounding*, Kant counters Hume's moral theory that implies morals are a question of taste, feeling, and sentiment, and change from person to person. For Hume, there are no moral facts, only moral opinions. Kant contends that Hume's line of thought suggests that God's justice, the ultimate divine moral law, is an illusion that causes people to live in error. Kant wants to move beyond a morality based on human nature to a universal system of moral judgment that binds all rational beings under all circumstances.

In order to formulate his moral system, Kant's earlier division of the cosmos into two realms, the noumenal (metaphysical world), and the phenomenal (physical world), is foundational. The noumenal realm is where Kant constructs his conception of the self as a free and autonomous being. The phenomenal world he concedes to the law of cause and effect and the limitations of determinism. In the world of phenomena, freedom is impossible because each event is caused by the event that precedes it. Kant's notion of the self has a dual nature—one very similar to Descartes's mind-body dualistic self—except the two aspects are not completely severed. Kant's self is one being, functioning in two realms. In one realm, it experiences freedom, a transcendental object; while in the other realm, it experiences dependence. Kant conceptualizes freedom as a complete idea, comprised of equally reciprocal, unified parts that are mutually exclusive yet mutually dependent. Basically, freedom is composed of determinism and independence ([1781] 1990). He contends that freedom is impossible without dependence.

Freedom empowers the rational being to will actions for itself. An autonomous will is essential to Kant's moral law. He defines the self as a rational agent endowed with a soul that is attuned with a moral sense. In the *Grounding*, Kant illustrates through reason how a "good will" can bring forth the "highest good." In the second *Critique*, he explains the practical dimensions of this process. "The establishment of a good will" is reason's highest practical function ([1785] 1983, 9). Only a rational being with a good will can bring forth the highest good (Kant [1788] 1993, 116–17). For Kant, the "highest good" may mean either the "perfect" highest good or the "supreme" highest good. The "*perfect* highest good" is a synthesis of virtue and happiness. The "*supreme* highest good," on the other hand, is the virtuous will. Kant asserts that our duty is not merely to bring forth a good will, but also to strive to bring forth the perfect highest good.

A human being, however, cannot bring forth the perfect highest good without pure practical reason. Kant writes:

> Only a rational being has the power to act according to his conception of laws, i.e., according to principles, and thereby has he a will … [t]he will is a faculty of choosing only that which reason, independently of inclination, recognizes as being practically necessary, i.e., as good. ([1785] 1983, 23)

Bringing forth the perfect highest good requires mastery over human nature. Because of humanity's limitations, it is impossible to know the motives upon which acts of virtue or duty rest (Kant [1785] 1983). Since the underlying motives of actions cannot be known, Kant provides a practical rule as the incentive for moral action. Morality itself, then, obligates a person with absolute necessity to act according to the moral law. Such moral acts occur according to the "categorical imperative" and promote the perfect highest good (Kant [1785] 1983, 30).

Kant formulates the categorical imperative as an imperative that obligates all moral agents. The categorical imperative obligates rational beings according to the maxim that can at the same time be willed a universal law. Kant assumes all rational beings implicitly recognize the existence of moral rules. Warner A. Wick, in *Immanuel Kant: Ethical Philosophy*, writes that Kant's "morality demands that we act on the sort of policies which, if adopted by everyone, would generate a community of free and equal members, each of whom in the process of realizing his own purposes also further the aims of his fellows" (Kant [1785] 1983, xv). When the agent does not submit to the universal moral rule, he or she succumbs to heteronomy, i.e., giving in to desires and passions or following the orders of external authority. Arbitrary exception to the universal moral rule also is an example of heteronomy. For Kant, when the agent is lured by desires, it is not free. Free behavior is rational, moral behavior. Not only does the self lose its freedom when it behaves heteronomously, but failure to adhere to the categorical imperative means doing that which is wrong or evil. On the other hand, by adhering to the categorical imperative, the self behaves freely, rationally, and autonomously and lives up to the moral law and is considered virtuous.

Kant posits that rational beings possess a will "independent of empirical conditions" and "determined [a priori] by the mere form of law" (Beck 1960, 177–80). The moral law forces itself upon us as an a priori proposition and is considered a "fact of pure practical reason" because "it proclaims itself as originating law" (Kant [1788] 1993, 31–32). In other words, once conscious of the moral law, a rational agent will self-legislate actions and conduct, executing them as duties, according to the categorical imperative. The moral law is instilled as a sense of duty (Kant [1793] 1934, 139) and has positive effects on individual and group behavior. This is especially important because the perfect highest good "cannot be achieved merely by the exertions of the single individual toward his own moral perfection, but requires rather a union of such individuals into a whole toward the same goal" ([1793] 1934, 89).

Kant postulates the existence of God as a necessary idea belonging to the perfect highest good ([1788] 1993). In *Kant's Conception of God*, England writes, "Kant speaks of God as 'a mere Idea of reason,' only to emphasize the point that 'God is not an object of the senses, but of reason alone,'" (1986 200). Yet, Kant maintains that "we are not only entitled but compelled to posit a real object corresponding to the Idea," God, "which for ever eludes our faculty of apprehension" (207). Kant writes: "[I]n the practical task of pure reason, i.e., in the necessary endeavor after the highest good, such a connection is postulated as necessary: we *ought* to seek to further the highest good" ([1788] 1993, 131).

According to Kant, we must construct an Ultimate Being if "we are to do full justice to all the facts of experience" (England 1986, 208). He contends that there is "a notion of an infinite ground [that] is required to supplement what is apprehended in and through sense-perception, in order that our conception and our systematization of the world of reality may be complete" (208). In addition, if we can conceive of the "best world" that can possibly be realized by our actions, there must be a perfect highest good, i.e., God, which is the cause of human nature. Attaining a sense of the nature of God is the result of a two-way process: the Supreme Creator of human nature manifests itself through human understanding (receptivity from God) and will (activity towards God) (Kant [1788] 1993, 132).

Though we cannot attain full knowledge of God, "we are endowed with awareness of a 'categorical imperative,' the voice within us of moral obligation, that when obeyed signifies our acknowledgment of a moral lawgiver" (Clements 1991, 11). God is conceived as an inference from the universal moral law to which the self, or rational agent, should willingly submit. In doing so, the self becomes a free, virtuous, responsible agent. Kant believes freedom is the activity of voluntarily submitting to a moral law. Rational beings are responsible moral agents, and it becomes their duty to live virtuously, since they are endowed with souls. Kant wants these rational agents to live up to their potential as soul-bearing beings in the phenomenal and noumenal realms. The categorical imperative is designed to help them do just that.

Pure reason, which operates only in the noumenal realm, is just half of the transcendental dialectic. If rational agents are to reach their potential, then practical reason also is necessary. Practical reason manifests itself in our actions in the world. In the phenomenal realm, inferences from the moral law are made about metaphysical concepts such as God, freedom, and immortality (Kant [1793] 1934, li). It is from the phenomenal perspective that Kant believes metaphysical concepts can have a powerful regulative effect on human behavior. To do this, he circumscribes God to the noumenal realm, where God is the moral lawgiver behind his categorical imperative and remains inconceivable to the human mind.

In the phenomenal realm, Kant contends that we cannot transcend the limits of experience. Our modes of thought are restricted by basic rules of understanding. We are only able to understand objects that appear in ordinary experience. Earlier, Kant referred to transcendental objects as noumena, objects that can be thought but not experienced. How do we come to understand objects that exist beyond sensory experience as transcendental objects? Since these objects are not part of our everyday worldly experience, the basic rule of causation does not apply to them. It is this limitation of knowledge that is placed upon human understanding that leads Kant to state that he has "limit[ed] reason to make room for faith" (Clements 1991, 11).

Humans have a need to speculate about the existence of transcendental objects. While we cannot experience them or know them as things-in-themselves, we are able to think of them as such, in order that they may play a role in the improvement of our lives in the world. The inability to know transcendental objects empirically should not be discouraging. Kant contends that the essence of our deepest powers has always been concealed from us. Neither should the lack of knowledge about transcendental objects limit our ability to postulate, conceive, and believe in them. They motivate us to act morally in practical matters and human activity.

Acting morally depends in large part on one's predisposition and disposition. Kant begins his *Religion within the Limits of Reason Alone* by establishing that the predisposition of human beings, which exists in the soul prior to birth, is neither good nor bad. In fact, Kant believes human beings are just "as much the one as

the other, partly good, partly bad" (Kant [1793] 1934, cxxvii).
Kant divides predisposition into three fundamental elements of
character and destiny. They are:

(1) Animality: which may be considered a "physical and purely
    mechanical self-love."
(2) Humanity: which reveals itself in "a self-love which is
    physical and yet *compares* with others" leading to jealousy
    and rivalry.
(3) Personality: which causes man to be "taken as a rational
    and at the same time an *accountable* being" that has the
    capacity to respect the moral law within him (Kant [1793]
    1934, 21–23).

Good and evil lie not in human nature but in human choices,
which ultimately determine character and disposition (Kant [1793]
1934, 17). If a person chooses an action based on a maxim that
incorporates the moral law, he or she has a good disposition. The
ability to have free will is vital to morality. According to Kant, this
is critical because incentives influence the will and can determine
the choices human beings make. The moral law also is an incentive,
and "whoever makes [the moral law] his maxim is *morally* good"
(Kant [1793] 1934, 19–20). Kant is attempting to develop a moral
law that would provide an incentive for rational beings to make
good choices and thus experience freedom.

Rational agents freely adopt their disposition by the choices
they make. According to Kant, "we are unable to derive … [the
disposition's] ultimate ground, from any original act of the will,"
thus the disposition is "a property of the will which belongs to it by
nature" and is ultimately "grounded in freedom" (Kant [1793] 1934,
20). The propensity of the self toward evil is the manifestation

of three distinct features: the *frailty* of human nature, *impurity* resulting from mixing immoral with moral motivating causes, and the propensity to adopt evil maxims as a result of *wickedness* in nature (Kant [1793] 1934, 24).

Earlier in Kant's life, he rejected the notion of rational beings acting heteronomously. Later, however, we see a fundamental shift in his interpretation of which acts are actually heteronomous. Acting according to the moral law appears heteronomous. In his attempt to purify his moral theory of heteronomy and strengthen his notion of moral duty, he redefines what was once considered heteronomous by relabeling choices based on transcendent ideas (or external incentives) as modes of expressing freedom (Kant [1793] 1934, lxv, lxxxix). For Kant, freedom brings responsibility. He asserts that a rational autonomous being, or self, must be responsible for who and what he becomes. The condition of the self "must be an effect of ... free choice; for otherwise he could not be held responsible for it and could therefore be *morally* neither good nor evil" (Kant [1793] 1934, 40). The self becomes either good or evil by the free choices made.

Kant admits that the task of continuously making good choices, while constantly assessing one's moral standing, is not easy. Since heteronomy is considered irresponsible, self-appraisal is necessary and noble.

> But in the judgment of men, who can appraise themselves and the strength of their maxims only by the ascendancy which they win over their sensuous nature in time, this change must be regarded as nothing but an ever-during struggle toward the better, hence as a gradual reformation

of the propensity to evil, the perverted cast of
mind. (Kant [1793] 1934, 43)

Stated differently, "man's moral growth of necessity begins not in
the improvement of his practices but rather in the transforming of
his cast of mind and in the grounding of a character" (Kant [1793]
1934, 43). "[T]he predisposition is thus gradually transformed into
a cast of mind, and *duty*, for its own sake, begins to have a noticeable
importance in their hearts" (44).

Then how does a man who has transformed his cast of mind deal
with the guilt of all of his past transgressions? Kant admits that
"history ... cries ... loudly" ([1793] 1934, 15) because of humanity's
evil deeds. Guilt is infinite (66).

> Whatever a man may have done in the way of
> adopting a good disposition, and indeed, however
> steadfastly he may have persevered in conduct
> conformable to such a disposition, he *nevertheless
> started from evil*, and this debt he can by no
> possibility wipe out. (Kant [1793] 1934, 66)

The guilt that arises from evil acts cannot be relieved through
grace or atonement. Kant writes that such sins are "*the most
personal of all debts*" and "only the culprit can bear" no matter how
"magnanimous" another may be and "wish to take [the debt] upon
himself for the sake of" the transgressor (Kant [1793] 1934, 66).
Kant explains:

> The extent of this guilt is due not so much to the
> *infinitude* of the Supreme Lawgiver whose authority
> is thereby violated (for we understand nothing

of such transcendent relationships of man to the
Supreme Being) as to the fact that this moral evil
lies in the *disposition* and the maxims in general, in
universal basic principles rather than in particular
transgressions. (Kant [1793] 1934, 66)

Each human being is his or her own lawgiver, moral tribunal, judge,
and savior. Each stands before him- or herself as a divine judge and
bears responsibility for the guilt of sins or the morality of actions.
Kant uses the life of Jesus as the model for this notion. He writes:
As his own "*savior* He renders satisfaction to supreme justice by His
sufferings and death; and as *advocate* He makes it possible for men
to hope to appear before their judge as justified" ([1793] 1934, 69).
Kant refers here to the Son of God as the archetypal figure for all
rational moral agents. Jesus's human nature consisted of a will, a
disposition, and a life that conformed to the same laws as any other
moral agent's. Kant claims that Jesus is his own lawgiver, judge, and
savior and a perfect example of a rational being adhering to the
categorical imperative. The highest legislation of nature must lie
within ourselves when we are attuned to the universal moral law.

For Kant, reason has a natural ability to seek out absolute, universal,
and necessary claims and principles upon which actions are based.
Kant's rational being shuns actions based on desires and passions
and opts for virtuous, moral behavior informed by practical
reason. But Kant fails to highlight adequately the instability and
uncertainty associated with continuously following one's duty to
the moral law. While each moral agent has a good will, reason does
not ensure right action. At any point, a moral agent may choose to
act on desires, passions, and self-interests and revert to less-than-
moral behavior. Every disposition has the propensity for good or
ill, and some individuals who were once moral may choose to act

badly. Self-judgment then becomes a problem. The immoral person acts evilly without the threat of external punishment. In addition, Kant's focus on the source and responsibility of evil in the choices of human beings leads to the failure to place adequate emphasis on the acts of transgression, while minimizing at best and overlooking at worst the impact of evil on others.

Given Kant's stance against giving in to passions and desires (heteronomy), he believes that rational agents will be responsible for judging their own bad and malicious behavior. He advocates for everyone bearing the burdens of their own evil deeds. But this belief is naïve and unrealistic because sometimes guilt is not enough to alter bad behavior for good behavior, and self-indictment is not an acceptable option for some agents. This aspect of Kant's moral theory essentially eliminates the threat of punishment from an external source, which is necessary if justice is to be administered on behalf of victims and society. While it appears that Kant is affording evil free rein, one must recall that he contends that freedom only exists in the noumenal realm. His theories are based on the belief that rational beings have a moral inclination and are aware of the categorical imperative. But, sometimes the categorical imperative is not enough to alter behavior for the good. *Ought* does not necessarily mean *will*. Yet, Kant believes rational beings will act morally and self-legislate their actions in both a noumenal and a phenomenal sense. He recognizes that in the world of phenomena, the law of cause and effect is operative, and agents are subject to the consequences of their actions. Kant's claims for self-legislation, self-appraisal, and self-punishment are unpractical because he is unable to achieve his aim in the physical world, no matter how much he attempts to illustrate it in theory.

If man is his own lawgiver, moral tribunal, divine judge, and savior, how does Kant understand the role of God in human lives? Kant writes in the *Religion*, "It concerns us not so much to know what God is in Himself (His nature)," as to "what He is for us as moral beings" ([1793] 1934, 130). For moral beings to know God, they

> must conceive and comprehend all the attributes of the divine nature (for instance, the unchangeableness, omniscience, omnipotence, etc. of such a Being) which, in their totality, are requisite to the carrying out of the divine will in this regard. Apart from this context we can know nothing about him. ([1793] 1934, 130–31)

Yet, for practical reasons, rational moral beings have chosen to believe in a transcendental God, whom they cannot comprehend but still describe as the omnipotent Creator, the holy legislator, the preserver of the human race, and the benevolent ruler (Kant [1793] 1934, 131).

Kant contends that God is an archetypal figure conceived of by rational beings, who transcendentally reflect divine attributes, developed out of experience and limitation. Kant continues:

> Faith in [God], regarded as an extension of the theoretical knowledge of the divine nature, would be merely the acknowledgment of a symbol of ecclesiastical faith which is quite incomprehensible to men or which, if they think they can understand it, would be anthropomorphic, and therefore nothing whatever would be accomplished for moral betterment. Only that which, in a practical context,

> can be thoroughly understood and comprehended,
> but which, taken theologically ... transcends all
> our concepts, is a mystery. ([1793] 1934, 133)

Although Kant argues that it is impossible for humans to comprehend what God is, he admits, "God has ... [sufficiently] revealed His will through the moral law in us" ([1793] 1934, 135). This great mysterious God "can be made comprehensible to each man through his reason as a practical and necessary religious idea" (135). A shift in Kant's conception of God takes place when "instead of arguing from duty to God by way of the *Summum Bonum* [highest good]," he contends that "in man's moral experience [he finds] a God who reveals Himself [to him] in and through the moral law" (lxvi). In other words, Kant contends that God reveals himself to the autonomous man in moral experience (receptivity), while in an almost simultaneous moment of consciousness, man infers God through moral sense (activity). In this moment of awakening, man is liberating himself from his desires and passions and moving toward maturity (Clements 1991, 10).

Finally, Kant argues that once the idea of God is comprehended, God exists, and moral agents take on qualities that are in common with God. This claim, in essence, counters Hume's assertion against supporters of natural theology, those adhering to the argument from design. Hume maintains that there is no analogy between human intelligence and supreme intelligence. He contends that this claim is baseless. Kant, on the other hand, affords the argument some credence. He asserts that from the definition of God, one already has an idea of a divine being in mind. If there is cosmological evidence that fits the description and conception held in mind, Kant contends that the argument from design has merit.

13

Schleiermacher's Feeling Self

LIKE KANT, FRIEDRICH DANIEL Ernst Schleiermacher (1768–1834) was born in Prussia and raised in a pietistic atmosphere. His family adhered to the beliefs and practices of the Moravian Brethren. Schleiermacher's father was a chaplain in the Prussian army. The Prussian ethos was socially, religiously, and theologically conservative. Under the leadership of Frederick William II and Frederick William III, the state supported repression of unorthodox religious and theological thought. It was during the reign of Frederick William III, who assumed leadership in 1797, that Kant failed to gain approval for the publication of three of the four books that were to comprise the *Religion*. During this time, Schleiermacher, like Kant, hoped for greater academic and religious freedom.

Schleiermacher's studies ranged from classical languages and mathematics to theology, philosophy, and classical philology. While at the University of Halle, he read Kant and would later take issue with a number of claims in his moral theory. Schleiermacher's first book, *On Religion: Speeches to Its Cultural Despisers* (1799), was in part a response to Kant's moral philosophy. Schleiermacher's understanding of religion is deeply influenced by Moravian, Enlightenment, and Romantic thought. These influences permeate his work.

Religion, writes Schleiermacher, "is the sensibility and taste for the infinite" ([1799] 1988, 103). It infuses life into all human and other finite forms of existence. Religion is the infinite, breathing into one and all, from the individual to the whole. Religion is the recognition that everything finite signifies the infinite; it is understanding that the temporal is an aspect of the eternal. Schleiermacher further explains:

> [T]o complete the general picture of religion, recall that every intuition is, by its very nature, connected with a feeling. Your senses mediate the connection between the object and yourselves; the same influence of the object, which reveals its existence to you. ([1799] 1988, 109)

While Schleiermacher believes that the objective of religion, metaphysics, and morals is the same: "the universe and the relationship of humanity to it" ([1799] 1988, 97), he nevertheless contends that the line of demarcation is breached when aspects of metaphysics and morality assimilate into religion and vice versa. Schleiermacher aims to rectify the distortion by differentiating religion from metaphysical claims and moral theory. He wants to distinguish religion from practical reason and transcendental philosophy. He maintains that these belief systems mistakenly minimize reality, falsely divide the universe and self into phenomenal and noumenal dimensions, and erroneously use reason to imply the existence of the ultimate. While Schleiermacher believes that religion tempers yet elevates speculation (metaphysics and transcendental philosophy) and praxis (moral activity and practical reasoning) above what they would otherwise be, he argues that religion:

> renounces ... all claims to whatever belongs to those others and gives back everything that has been forced upon it. It does not wish to determine and explain the universe according to its nature as does metaphysics; it does not desire to continue the universe's development and perfect it by the power of freedom and the divine free choice of a human being as does morals. Religion's essence is neither thinking nor acting, but intuition and feeling. (Schleiermacher [1799] 1988: 102)

Schleiermacher believes the infinite universe ceaselessly acts upon human beings. He contends that the universe continually beckons us to awaken to our source of life as individuals. The call of the universe is recognized as *intuition* and *feeling*. *Intuition*, according to Schleiermacher, is knowledge without intellectually organizing activity. It is an awareness, though not embedded in the ordinary cognizing activity of the intellect. Intuition is initiated by "felt resistance," and from this action upon us, our sense perception proceeds to make us aware of the infinite. "All intuition proceeds from an influence of the intuited on the one who intuits, from an original and independent action of the former, which is then grasped, apprehended, and conceived by the latter according to one's own nature" (Schleiermacher [1799] 1988, 104).

Every intuition of the universe is accompanied by a feeling. The intensity of the feeling is directly related to the degree of intuition. *Feeling* is that sense that accompanies all perceptions, insights, revelations, and religious intuitions. Feeling resonates throughout the whole of one's being and accompanies all acts of consciousness. *Feeling*, according to Schleiermacher, is described as "a basic or primal awareness of the self in relation to 'the universe'" (Clements 1991, 23). "Intuition without feeling is nothing and can have neither the proper origin nor the proper force; feeling without intuition is also nothing; both are therefore something only when and because they are originally one and unseparated" (Schleiermacher [1788] 1988, 112).

"Religion knows no other means to that final goal than that it expresses and imparts itself freely," writes Schleiermacher. "When religion stirs with all its own power, when in the flow of this movement it sweeps along with it every faculty of one's mind into its service, it thus also expects to penetrate to the innermost being of every individual who breathes its atmosphere" ([1799] 1988, 141). According to Schleiermacher, every person is born with a religious capacity and should engage in every aspect of life from a religious vantage point. Religion directs all life outward toward the universe, the primary aim of which is relation with humanity. "[F]or in order to intuit the world and to have religion, man must first have found humanity, and he finds it only in love and through love … Humanity itself is actually the universe" (120).

Since humanity is the universe, each individual is a compendium of all humanity, and access to the universe is thereby through other human beings. Mediators are required to activate, for each self-conscious being, the capacity to be religious. To be religious in isolation, asserts Schleiermacher, is impossible. To be human and self-conscious is to be conscious of one's relationship to others. Intuition into the universe is, therefore, social and historical. In the social context, each individual is dependent upon another to awaken him or her to the infinite; in the historical context, each individual is unable to properly grasp his or her role in history without a stream of consciousness and understanding of self in relation to others. While Schleiermacher's notion of the self emerges out of a social context, it also is founded on the "principle of individuation." This principle is based on the belief that the universe yields entities that cannot be divided. Human beings are individuated, each self possessing individuality, i.e., material and physical uniqueness, the inability to replicate one's essence, and a stream of consciousness solely one's own.

Self-consciousness, asserts Schleiermacher, is the simultaneous awareness of self and the consciousness of the changing state of being in which one finds him- or herself. In every moment of consciousness, there is a self-caused element, which Schleiermacher labels *activity* and a nonself-caused element, labeled *receptivity*.

> Thus in every self-consciousness there are two elements, which we might call respectively a self-caused element ... and a non-self-caused element...; or Being and a Having-by-some-means-come-to-be ... the latter of these presupposes for every self-consciousness another factor besides the Ego, a factor which is the source of the particular determination, and without which the self-consciousness would not be precisely what it is ... [T]he double constitution of self-consciousness causes us always to look objectively for an Other to which we can trace the origin of our particular state ... In self-consciousness there are only two elements: the one expresses the existence

of the subject for itself, the other its co-existence
with an Other. (Schleiermacher [1830] 1989, 13)

Consciousness in the world is a two-way mode of mediation
between the self and God, and it is from this relationship that piety
is awakened. It is through piety, or as *feeling*, that one becomes
conscious of God's divine call to revealed religion (Schleiermacher
[1830] 1989, 8). Self-consciousness, for Schleiermacher, is a way of
understanding one's life in this world. To cognitively penetrate the
innermost sanctuary of life is to feel and understand the power of
one's relationship to the infinite. He writes:

> Life … is to be conceived as an alternation between
> an abiding-in-self … and a passing-beyond-self …
> on the part of the subject. The two forms of
> consciousness (Knowing and Feeling) constitute
> the abiding-in-self, while Doing proper is the
> passing-beyond-self. … Knowing and Feeling
> stand together in antithesis to Doing. But while
> Knowing, in the sense of possessing knowledge,
> is an abiding-in-self on the part of the subject,
> nevertheless as the act of knowing, it only becomes
> real by a passing-beyond-self of the subject, and in
> this sense it is a Doing. ([1830] 1989, 8)

While the self must alternate between the activities of abiding-in-
self and passing-beyond-self, piety, according to Schleiermacher,
is constitutive to abiding-in-self as *feeling*. Consciousness of the
self lies at the core of every human activity where piety or *feeling*
informs the activities of life by stimulating knowing and doing.

> Accordingly an action (a Doing) will be pious in so
> far as the determination of self-consciousness, the
> feeling which had become affective and had passed
> into a motive impulse, is a pious one ... Thus both
> hypotheses lead to the same point: that there are
> both a Knowing and a Doing which pertain to
> piety, but neither of these constitutes the essence
> of piety." (Schleiermacher [1830] 1989, 10)

The two-way mode of mediation between the self and God is comprised of *receptivity* and *activity*. The self is itself because of its coexistence with and codependence on others. The mode of activity would be impossible without the counter impulse of receptivity. Activity without an object upon which to focus would leave acts without direction and produce chaos in the universe. "But as we never do exist except along with an Other, so even in every outward-tending self-consciousness the element of receptivity, in some way or other affected, is the primary one" (Schleiermacher [1830] 1989, 13).

The two-way mode of mediation forms an essential element of Schleiermacher's theological thought. With the opposing impulses within the self, Schleiermacher takes on Kant's moral philosophy. Kant contends that causation renders freedom impossible in the phenomenal realm, but transcendental freedom is possible in the noumenal, which is beyond the law of cause and effect. Kant then maintains that each self, though unified in existence, can function in two separate spheres. Schleiermacher argues that pure freedom does not exist in any aspect of human nature. He contends that claims of absolute freedom are deceptive, especially the transcendental type. He holds that the self cannot be separated into two halves: phenomenal and noumenal. Human nature proves this duality a falsehood. Dependence and freedom, Schleiermacher argues, are bound together within each person. This unity means that any *feeling* of freedom is constrained by dependence. Freedom and dependence are mutually dependent experiences; neither can exist without the other, and therefore each limits the other.

The feeling of dependence is characterized by receptivity, and the feeling of freedom by activity, asserts Schleiermacher. The source of self-consciousness is from an influence outside the self. It is for this reason that a feeling of dependence accompanies the receptive state. Each self is dependent upon external influences for existence. While life depends on a source external to itself, all of life is not defined by the state of dependence.

Activity, according to Schleiermacher, affords the feeling of freedom. Yet, because freedom permeates our whole existence, it eventually encounters its antithesis and is constrained by dependence. Absolute freedom is always consciousness of absolute dependence. Without dependence, freedom is impossible.

This two-way mode of mediation has a direct relationship to God, explains Schleiermacher:

> As regards the identification of absolute dependence with "relation to God" in our proposition: this is to be understood in the sense that the *Whence* of our receptive and active existence, as implied in this self-consciousness, is to be designated by the word "God," and that this is for us the really original significance of that word. (Schleiermacher [1830] 1989, 16)

Consciousness of a feeling of dependence upon a higher source is, therefore, the same as being in relation with God.

While "this feeling of dependence is itself conditioned by some previous knowledge about God" ([1830] 1989, 17), arising out of one's social context, the word *God* presupposes any corresponding idea that is merely "the expression of the feeling of absolute dependence," contends Schleiermacher, which is "the most direct reflection upon [God]" (Clements 1991, 104).

Schleiermacher explains:

> God signifies for us simply that which is the co-determinant in this feeling and to which we trace our being in such a state ... Now this is just what is principally meant by the formula which says that to feel oneself absolutely dependent and to be conscious of being in relation with God are one and the same thing; and the reason is that absolute dependence is the fundamental relation which must include all others in itself. ([1830] 1989, 17)

Schleiermacher's conception of God is not to be understood as a supreme idea derived from moral obligation, nor as an analogy to human intellect. Neither should Schleiermacher's notion of God be viewed "in isolation as some self-contained element of the human consciousness" (Clements 1991, 36). Schleiermacher's conception of God emerges out of an understanding of the self-in-relation to the other. Our relation to "the other" is based on sense experience. As we intuit an object, it is connected to a *feeling*. Schleiermacher's understanding of *feeling* and self-consciousness are interrelated. He writes: "[Our] senses mediate the connection between the object and [ourselves]; the same influence of the object, which reveals its existence to [us], must stimulate [our senses] in various ways and produce a change in [our] inner consciousness" ([1799] 1988, 109).

Schleiermacher's notion of God is an awareness of a *feeling* awakened in us by the infinite. He conceives of God as the ordering force upon which the finite and infinite relate. His conception of God is characterized by a highly personal inward experience. "God is given to us in feeling in an original way," writes Schleiermacher ([1830] 1989, 17). The *givenness* should not be confused with God in any way being given from a place outside of us,

> because anything that is outwardly given must be given as an object exposed to our counter-influence, however slight this may be. The transference of the idea of God to any perceptible object, unless one is all the time conscious that it is a piece of purely arbitrary symbolism, is always a corruption. (Schleiermacher [1830] 1989: 18)

Schleiermacher's notion of *givenness* never exists outside human nature. It is innate in the interpenetration of the infinite life force that permeates all existence. There is no existence without life, therefore, the finite and the infinite are one, and self-consciousness and God-consciousness are the same.

According to Schleiermacher, God-consciousness and self-consciousness both awaken a "feeling of absolute dependence." Says Clements, "This might be better expressed as 'the feeling of being utterly dependent,'" since knowing God is not only relational but communal (1991, 99). The feeling awakens us to the emotional nature of religion, which is embodied in a social context where the individual gains awareness of self and others, including society and the universe. God-consciousness is expressed as receptivity from an external source that prompts a *feeling of dependence* and an internal spontaneous activity that inspires a *feeling of freedom* (Clements 1991).

Consciousness of the world is "the medium through which the infinite God is acting upon us" (Clements 1991, 38). Human beings live in and through God, just as God lives in and through human beings. This sense of interrelatedness is the medium through which God is revealed, provoking a feeling of utter dependence. All experience and all that is perceived through our senses depends upon God. Human beings, the world, and the universe are absolutely dependent upon God, and therefore even the law of causation is ordered *and* willed by God (Clements 1991), making freedom impossible, as Schleiermacher has argued.

With Schleiermacher, writes Keith W. Clements in *Friedrich Schleiermacher: Pioneer of Modern Theology,* "we are on the way to the modern refusal to speak of God as an object within the world ... but rather as the ground of all being" (1991, 53). God acts in all things, God's nature is revealed in all things, and God's will is expressed in every occurrence. In other words, Schleiermacher conceptualizes the infinite God as the ultimate life force, whose active presence wills and orders all things finite. God is the ground upon which all is dependent and the source of all things (Christian 1979). Dependence and determinism are reality in human nature. Freedom can merely be imagined in activity but never experienced in its pure form.

14

Summary: God, the Self and the Imagination

*I*N BOOK 2, WE have examined the manner in which God and the self are conceptualized and understood from the perspective of major thinkers in the Western philosophical tradition. The historical contexts in which the philosophers lived and the convergence of their views offer insights into how and why changes in these concepts occurred. Philosophical adversaries critiqued theological claims, postulations, and theoretical positions that were considered to have negative effects on individuals and in societies. Charges of erroneous notions, fictitious beliefs, and faulty assertions were not unusual. The philosophers featured in this work argued that deceptive beliefs and distorted thinking about God hinder the realization of self-responsibility and personal development, which ultimately stifles social responsibility and communal development.

In their efforts to help human beings self-actualize and realize their inherent genius, the philosophers in this book masterfully used imagination to invigorate their thoughts to make transcendental leaps back and forth between two alternate worlds, in order to overcome the burden of discontinuity, duality, and separateness

(Norton 1968). The philosophers employed imagination to bind distinct and disconnected ideas, feelings, and sensations into unified concepts of God and self. They envisioned "what [was] absent, unreal or even absurd, and so [imagination] appears to grant [them] almost unlimited conceptual powers" (Beaney 2016, 49).

According to the *Dictionary of Philosophy of Mind,* Aristotle first introduced the concept of imagination into philosophy. The term 'imagination' has Latin roots in the word *imaginatio.* (Thomas 2004) While the definitions of imagination are nuanced and many, this work defines imagination as "the capacity that underpins our ability to simulate perspectives that differ from the one available to us through experience" (Liao and Gendler 2011, 79). All the philosophers in this book utilized their imaginations and constructively integrated imagination and creativity into their works allowing us to relish in their thoughts and the implications of their thinking and understanding. When thinking about current events and historical developments, these thinkers posited that the imagination is freer than knowledge and memory (Norton 1968, 404). The philosophers in this work demonstrated the powerful role of the imagination in unifying distinct percepts or "a loose collection of atomic particles (whether 'ideas' or 'sensation') which are simple, self-identical and presumably indubitable" (403). These particles are bound together as "conceptual and proposition unities ... in our knowledge ... [and] *imagination* is the glue" (403–404).

Yet, in the process of associating ideas, the philosophers controlled the "capricious fancy" of an otherwise unrestrained imagination and subjected imagination "to certain principles of knowledge" (Norton 1968, 404) essentially demanding imagination's obedience. They "rested human knowledge on this lawful imagination" (404) and "triumphantly brandished [imagination] as an autonomous means to a knowledge which is infinitely superior to ordinary knowledge" (405). The philosphers featured in this book effectively garnered the power of imagination to face and challenge traditional customs and beliefs, theological dogma, political oppression, and human suffering. The imagination was employed "to brush aside the utilitarian symbols, the conventional and socially accepted generalities, in short, everything that veils reality from us in order to bring us face to face with reality itself" (405).

Through the "activities of reason, feeling and perception which together make up bound consciousness" (Norton 1968, 407), the philosophers in this work parlayed imagination onto the center stage of their projects and elevated its philosophical importance in our understanding of God and the self.

The creative power of the imagination is necessary whenever one postulates and discusses the nature of God and the properties of the self. Descartes's project begins when he uses his imagination in effort to eliminate the external control of moral authority. His aim is to locate the authority for moral sources inward. He wants humanity to attain peace and find truth on its own through reason. To achieve his aim, he begins his exercise in doubting by discussing the manner in which the imagination is able to fashion concepts, either true or false, in the mind. At one point, he imagines that the objects around him, including his own body parts, do not exist. At another point, he is discussing an artist's ability to concoct the novel or paint the bizarre by combining different aspects of animals and objects (Descartes [1637] 1993, 61). Then, in another instance, after realizing that "he exists," he asks himself: "What else am I?" (65). Descartes replies: "I will set my imagination in motion" and "use my imagination in order to recognize more distinctly who I am" (65–66). His claim of mind-body dualism was criticized as an illusion made possible by the imagination. Some philosophers attacked the concept of separating self-consciousness from its embodiment as fictitious.

Locke believes that people, animals, and other objects possess natural properties and powers that are not being respected by governmental authority and others in power. He hopes to demolish all ideas, customs, traditions, and languages to establish that knowledge is based on experience. In doing this, he affirms ordinary life and overturns the hierarchical structure dominating social and political relations. His philosophical thought begins with the foundational elements of *simple* and *complex* ideas. Both are formulated by the imagination. Locke contends that simple ideas are uncompounded, containing "nothing but *one uniform Appearance*, or Conception in the mind" ([1689] 1975, 119). Complex ideas, on the other hand, result from "combining several simple *Ideas* into one compound one" (163). Locke leaves it to the imagination to deconstruct ideas in order to conceive that a mere simple idea actually exists. He then allows his imagination to go to work deconstructing and reconstructing ideas to grasp a complex idea.

Locke imagines that self-annihilation is possible by the self. It is necessary for the demolition of old beliefs and traditions, so that new beliefs, traditions, and customs can be constructed. He then postulates the complex idea, God. Since we have no innate ideas of God, he contends that we gain proof of God's existence through deductive reasoning. From our own finite existence, Locke deduces that *something* has existed for eternity. Through circular logic, Locke imagines an eternal being, known as God (Locke [1689] 1975, 623).

Hume believes humanity places too much faith in dogmas, mysteries, superstitions, customs and traditions—all lacking a "real" foundation. He hopes to open humanity's eyes to its fictitious beliefs. He seeks to accomplish this by criticizing claims based on sameness of self or identity of objects, such as God. He believes ideas based on the "principle of individuation" are deceptive and mere fiction. Hume acknowledges that the function of the imagination is necessary to separate and compile complex ideas, but the imagination simultaneously contributes to the deception by leading one to believe in identity, whether it be God, the self, a person, an object, or an idea. Hume contends that when we believe in *identity*, we believe a falsehood, because we are only able to know discrete perceptions.

Hume's skepticism prompts Kant to save humanity from a radical determinism on the one hand and existential annihilation on the other hand. To do this, Kant uses his imagination to posit freedom as a reality and to restore faith in God's existence. Kant divides the universe and the self into two dimensions: the phenomenal, where determinism rules, and the noumenal, where freedom is possible. Kant postulates a conception of God as a transcendental idea and uses his imagination to envisage piercing the moral law to imply God's existence as an object hidden from view. Kant's notion of the self is imagined as a unified rational being with the ability to function in both realms—reaching a level of genius.

Kant writes in the *Critique of Pure Reason*: "[Synthesis in general] is the mere result of the power of the imagination, a blind but indispensable function of the soul, without which we should have no knowledge whatsoever, but of which we are scarcely ever conscious" (Clements 1991, 138). Michael Beaney elaborates in *Imagination:*

The Missing Mystery of Philosophy (2016) that Kant "held that the imagination was fundamental to the human mind, not only bringing together our sensory and intellectual faculties but also acting in creative ways." Beaney further adds that Kant's conception of imagination "blossom[ed] in Romanticism and [found] poetic expression in the works of Coleridge and Wordsworth."

Finally, Schleiermacher aims to awaken a slumbering humanity to a better self and universe. To do this, he counters claims that God is an object, inference, or archetypal figure. He imagines God as an infinite spirit, a life force that is intuited from the universe. Schleiermacher uses the imagination to awaken a *feeling* within the finite to a feeling of total dependence upon an infinite force. This awakening also yields the sense of *freedom*. With the imagination, we experience a two-way process of mediation, impulses of receptivity and activity, between the finite and the infinite.

"Whether we have a God as part of our intuition depends on the direction of our imagination," writes Schleiermacher. "[The] imagination," he goes on to say, "is the highest and most original element in us, and that everything besides it is merely reflected upon it; you will know that it is your imagination that creates the world for you, and that you can have no God without the world" ([1799] 1988, 138).

In this book, we have gained greater appreciation for philosophical understandings of the imagination. The power of the imagination allows the mind to transcend reality and limitations, to move beyond would-be boundaries of thought and distinctions between what is real and unreal. The philosophers in this book demonstrate that "Imagination [or transcendental freedom] 'does not destroy or even insult Reason.' It grants to reason access to modes of meaning—possible worlds—alternative to that possibility which is presently accorded the status of actuality" (Norton 1968, 411).

Book 3

SELF-AWARENESS

15

Introduction: The Self and Pragmatism

*T*HE ESSAYS IN BOOK 3 seek to analyze the self from the perspectives of one's relationship to oneself and one's relationship to others. The analysis is largely informed by the works of two pragmatists, William James and George Herbert Mead. James offers the vantage point of a psychologist and Mead that of a social behaviorist. The essays examine the relationships of the self to consciousness, personality, habits, attention, language, social relations, and the environment. For insight and understanding of the concept of *personal identity*, the essay "The Self and Personal Identity" draws upon the works of John Locke and David Hume. In book 3, the following questions will be explored:

1. Of what is a self comprised?
2. What is the self's objective?
3. How does one come to know himself or herself?
4. What is the body's relationship to the self?
5. What is the relationship between the self and consciousness?
6. How does the self relate to other selves, objects, and ideas?
7. What is the relationship between the self and *personal identity*?

16

The Emergence of the Self

*T*HIS ESSAY IS DIVIDED into two parts. The first section examines the nature of the self as *I*, the knower, and *me*, the known. The examination is from psychological and social behaviorist viewpoints. The second section analyzes the emergence of the self and explains how it develops in the midst of experience.

Recognition of the self requires one to be aware of his or her *own* personal existence. In this state of awareness, where one is conscious of being a subject and an object, consciousness must be viewed as a function, not an entity, according to William James in his essay "Does 'Consciousness' Exist?" When one is conscious, one is *thinking*, and the function that thought performs in human experience is *knowing*. As conscious, thinking beings, we experience the world through sense perception. "Pure experience" is "the one primal stuff in the world," says James, and "[k]nowing can easily be explained as a particular sort of relation towards one another into which portions of pure experience may enter" ([1906] 1996, 4).

An essential aspect of consciousness is its unified nature in experience. What might appear to be two discrete elements (i.e., subject and object) in experience, is actually subject-plus-object (James [1906] 1996, 5). *"Experience ... has no such inner duplicity; and the separation of it into consciousness and content comes, not by way of subtraction, but by way of addition"* (9). In the self, these two "discriminated aspects" are considered to be partly knower *I* and partly known *me* (James [1892] 1985, 43). Although consciousness itself indicates an external relation, the experiences of knowing and known are not separate. The knower and the reality of the known are one. James wants to eliminate the artificially construed separation between subject and object that is said to exist united within the self. He argues that philosophy has inaccurately maintained a dualism between "discontinuous entities" ([1906] 1996, 23, 52).

James's notion of the self is analogous to jazz. Dr. Cornel West often lectured about the free-jazz form of John Coltrane, the great American saxophonist and composer, and his quartet. West highlighted the power and beauty of improvisation. Using jazz as a metaphor for the self, consider the music of John Coltrane, for example. The melodies and rhythms produced are unique to Coltrane and his instrument. The musician alone could not produce the jazz; neither could the instrument by itself. Thus, it is by way of addition and not subtraction that jazz emerges. The same is true for the self, the *I* and *me*. In the following pages, closer examination of the knower and the known will shed more light on the concept of transcending duplicity through addition.

James holds that "a man's Me is the sum total of all that he can call his" ([1892] 1985, 44). This includes his family, home and land, all other property and possessions, and beliefs, desires, and actions.

The *me* can be divided theoretically into three components: (1) the constituents, (2) feelings and emotions, and (3) responses and actions.

In reference to the constituents (the material, social, and spiritual *mes*), James writes: "The *body* is the innermost part of the material me in each of us; and certain parts of the body seem more intimately ours than the rest" ([1892] 1985, 44–45). Material objects such as clothing, family, the home, and other possessions also are aspects of the material me. The attention we receive through our interaction with others comprises the social *me*. Our desire for fame and recognition, whether positive or negative, motivates us to act in relation to others. The collection of one's states of consciousness, psychic faculties, and dispositions comprise the spiritual *me* (46–48).

Feelings and emotions are incited by constituents. As human beings relate to their constituents, the body experiences certain psychological and physiological impulses. These feelings and emotions are called *self-appreciation*. There are two types of self-appreciation: self-complacency, defined as "pride, conceit, vanity, self-esteem, arrogance, and vainglory;" and self-dissatisfaction, defined as "modesty, humility, confusion, diffidence, shame, mortification ... and personal despair" (James [1892] 1985, 49). In other words, human beings are known to be self-centered or selfish, since they can only view the world from their unique perspective. Self-seeking results as these feelings and emotions are experienced. James reveals that self-seeking can be divided into two parts: bodily and social. "[R]eflex actions and movements of alimentation and defense are acts of bodily self-seeking" (51). These actions can be prompted by fear and anger, and they can lead to the construction of shelter, the acquisition of food, and the care of loved ones. Our desire for attention and social recognition, our dispositions to love and hate, and the need for power and influence, all contribute to the impulses that lead to social self-seeking. The aim of these behavioral responses or actions is *self-preservation*.

The different *mes*, their feelings, emotions, and actions, may find themselves in conflict. Time constraints, space limitations, and restrictions from physical nature force the self to set priorities. We are able to manifest different selves because of varying interests at different times in our lives. What we can actually become, however, is limited, due to the selectivity of our attention. In life we are forced to make decisions about which actions to delay and objects to sacrifice, in order to achieve one's ideal self. These decisions are guided by self-interests and ensure the development of specific *mes*. Thus, it is self-interest that ultimately leads to the preservation of the self. Without being self-centered—or in other words, without the endowment of self-seeking impulses and the feelings of self-satisfaction—the self would perish (James [1892] 1985).

The *I* is aware of *itself* and its *personal existence*. It is the *thinker*. At any given moment, it is the *I* that is conscious of *me*. "Whereas the Me is only one of the things which [the *I*] is conscious *of*" (James [1892] 1985, 62–63). But what is the thinker? The answer to this question resides in the personal self.

The personal self is conscious of thoughts that belong to no other. Each personal self is a singular consciousness. It is connected to thoughts, and feeling them, it responds. Consciousness of thoughts manifests in the knowledge of one's *own* existence. James contends, "The first and foremost concrete fact which every one will affirm to belong to his inner experience is the fact that consciousness of some sort goes on" ([1892] 1985, 19). As consciousness goes on, thoughts rise out of and result from prior thoughts.

According to James, consciousness has four major characters. First, every "state" tends to be part of a personal consciousness. Thoughts are not exchanged between any two individuals. My thoughts are mine, and your thoughts are yours ([1892] 1985, 19). Second, within each personal consciousness, states are always changing. James further explains that: *"no state once gone can recur and be identical with what it was before,"* and *"there is no proof that an incoming current ever gives us just the same bodily sensation twice"* (21). The third character of personal consciousness is that it is sensibly continuous. The lack of breach, crack, or division is what makes consciousness continuous. Neither time gaps nor changes in the quality of consciousness prevent the feeling of sensible continuity (25). The last character of personal consciousness is interested in parts of its object to the exclusion of others. Personal consciousness, therefore, selectively attends to objects of interest (37–38).

As the mind is bombarded with an infinite array of objects, each human being personally selects and prioritizes objects of interest. This individualized approach to selection creates personal experiences and contributes to the formation of the personal self. Age, class, race, gender, health, religion, sexual orientation, cultural environment, etc., influence life experiences, which are "almost entirely determined by our habits of attention" (James [1892] 1985, 39). "What [a man] shall *become* is fixed by the conduct of this moment ... The problem with the man is less what act he shall now resolve to do than what being he shall now choose to become," writes James (41).

George Herbert Mead writes about the self in his book *Mind, Self, & Society*. He discusses the nature of the *I* and *me* (1934, 173–222). The self arises with the awareness of the *I* and *me* that results from a three-way conversational process operative within the individual. The *me* is that aspect of the self that assumes the attitudes of others toward itself. According to James, the *me* is objectified through its identification and resonance with objects. For Mead, however, the *me* is based on the attitudes appropriated from others. The appropriation of an organized set of attitudes derived from a social group gives way to the emergence of *me*. The *me* then beckons the *I*, which awakens and responds to it. But as quickly as the *I* reacts to the organized attitudes, it becomes the *me* to which it was responding. The *I*, therefore, is the individual organism's response to the *me*, which is the organized attitudes of others (1934, 173–78).

According to Mead, the *I* and *me* are separated in a triadic communication process: (1) the emergence of the *me* once it has assumed attitudes of the community; (2) the *me*'s call for a response; and (3) the reply of the *I*. He writes, "they belong together in the sense of being parts of a whole" (1934, 178). Mead explains that the self is "essentially a social process going on with … two distinguishable phases," the *I* and the *me* (178). The jazz metaphor is also appropriate here, however, in a different manner. The self, like jazz, emerges not by its *own* choice but manifests through the conjunctive relation between two distinct elements—the musician and the instrument— whose interrelationship and interaction predate the self's birth.

The content of human life and the impulses that drive the birth and development of the self are a function of conjunctive relations that become a part of our experience. James maintains in his essay "A World of Pure Experience" that the "content" of a human life is the natural process that leads us out of one experience into another. Whether the mind holds before it a name, a resemblance of an object, or a clear image, these percepts provide stimuli for movement. It is this process of moving out of one experience into another that leads to the creation of new selves.

According to James, the "sense of continuity" between moments is the "most intimate of all conjunctive relations" ([1906] 1996, 50). But what drives this sense of continuity in human beings? It is self-seeking, the need "to know." We have an innate desire to know things, and it is this inherent drive that ushers us forward from one moment of experience to the next and positions humans on the leading edge of thought and time. Human beings are endowed with mental and physical impulses that drive their behavior in relation to themselves, others, and the world.

Two examples from the Old Testament shed light on the abstract theory of conjunctive relations and also provide insight into how the self emerges. In the Bible, the most intimate relation between a subject and object, the knower and known, is expressed by the term "to know." Two such biblical passages that make reference to the physical union between a man (the knower) and a woman (the known) will help to illustrate this point: "Now Adam *knew* [italics mine] Eve his wife, and she conceived" (Genesis 4:1 NKJV); and "And Elkanah *knew* [italics mine] Hannah his wife, and the LORD remembered her" (1 Samuel 1:19 NKJV).

"Conjunctive experience" is symbolized in the intimate relation between a man and woman—the carriers of life. The "terminus" or end goal is the child conceived. Through conception, the man and woman—the "discriminated parts"—find unity in the same potential self, the child. The two distinct entities exist both separately and in the newly conceived. The newborn lacks inner duplicity, because the two parts that exist within the newborn exist by way of addition and not subtraction.

The child, or percept, is the object "in mind." Prior to birth, there is only knowledge—about the unborn child in the womb. During pregnancy, the knowing is in transit. The parents are *virtual* knowers of the unborn child. They proceed to act on their knowledge and experience as long as their thinking goes unchallenged (James [1906] 1996). After the birth of the child, the parents experience the knowledge of acquaintance. Knowing is verified and complete. One can now better appreciate the statement, "Where direct acquaintance is lacking, 'knowledge about' is the next best thing" (73).

After the birth of the child, the newborn does not cease being a percept, according to Mead, who defines *percept* as an image or physical object that "is a construct in which the sensuous stimulation is merged with imagery which comes from past experience" (1964, 134). However, Mead contends that a newborn is not a self. The self is born out of social processes and is developed in and through social interaction, in which language is vital. A newborn lacks the ability to distinguish parts of her body from the objects around her. The infant is incapable of knowing that her hands or feet are part of her body. She is unaware of herself.

The self begins to develop when she is able to make the distinction between herself and her surroundings. Mead argues that it is through language that the individual becomes an object to herself (1934, 135, 138). A conversation of gestures facilitates the social process. He describes the process of communication in terms of its

> triadic relation on which the existence of meaning
> is based: the relation of the gesture of one organism
> to the adjusted response made to it by another
> organism, in its indicative capacity as pointing to
> the completion or resultant of the act it initiates.
> (1934, 145)

The meanings of gestures, claims Mead, are derived from the responses of other organisms. These meanings cannot be determined from the acts of a single individual that is isolated from all social relations. Experiences with others always predate and facilitate the arrival of any self. Community and social processes are, therefore, prerequisites for the emergence of the self. Mead maintains that he knows "of no other form of behavior than the linguistic in which the individual is an object to himself, and, so far as [he] can see, the individual is not a self in the reflexive sense unless he is an object to himself" (1934, 142).

Individuals within a social environment must develop symbols to facilitate the communication process. An actor must learn or develop signs that will arouse in others the feelings, emotions, behaviors, and expressions that he or she is experiencing. To complete the triadic relationship, the symbol must return to the actor and arouse in him or her that which it awakened in the other individuals. Mead explains that Helen Keller lacked the mental content of herself, until she was able to communicate with others using symbols that stirred in her the reactions they aroused in others (Mead 1934, 149). As young children interact with their peers, adults, and imaginary companions, a conversation of gestures stimulates the development of a self within the child as he or she assumes the roles of others. Mead reveals that the child develops:

a set of stimuli which call out in himself the sort
of responses they call out in others ... Such is the
simplest form of being another to one's self ... The
child says something in one character and responds
in another character, and then his responding in
another character is a stimulus to himself in the
first character, and so the conversation goes on.
(1934, 151)

It is through social processes, such as assuming the roles and values
of others, and through the use of language that a child develops the
capabilities to interact and function as a self. Self-consciousness is
critical to the realization of the self, explains Mead:

[W]hat we mean by self-consciousness is an
awakening in ourselves of the group of attitudes
which we are arousing in others ... It is unfortunate
to fuse or mix up consciousness, as we ordinarily use
that term, and self-consciousness. Consciousness,
as frequently used, simply has reference to the
field of experience, but self-consciousness refers
to the ability to call out in ourselves a set of definite
responses which belong to the others of the group.
(1934, 163)

As the self develops, the individual is better able to get outside
of himself. He eventually comes to know the difference between
himself and the objects that surround him. The ability to think
intelligently and rationally about oneself is an aspect of selfhood
and self-consciousness. The individual must be able to take an
objective account of himself and his environment; meanwhile, his

body and the objects comprising the material environment around his body, though changing constantly, remain continuous percepts.

"The objective nucleus of every [person's] experience, [one's] own body, is ... a continuous percept; and equally continuous as a percept ... is the material environment of that body, changing by gradual transition when the body moves" (James [1906] 1996, 65). Around the body, or the nucleus, floats a cloud of shared experience. The objects and experiences of our world are partly shared and common and partly discrete and distinct.

The desire of human beings to know propels humanity forward. James writes: "These are what the unions are *worth*, these are all that *we can ever practically mean* by union, by continuity" (1996, 59). James further states:

> So much for the essentials of the cognitive relation, where the knowledge is conceptual in type, or forms knowledge "about" an object. It consists in intermediary experiences ... of continuously developing progress, and finally, of fulfilment, when the sensible percept, which is the object, is reached. ([1906] 1996, 60)

17

The Self and Personality

EACH INDIVIDUAL SELF HAS a personality that is uniquely its own. Personality is defined as "a 'stable set of tendencies and traits' [and] the behavior—thoughts, feelings, and actions—that distinguishes [a person] from others," (Gills 2004, 95). Personality arises through the process of self-realization, which occurs in both psychological and social processes. Personality is continually constituted as the self experiences its inner and outer environments. Factors such as physical and mental health, family, spiritual life, geographical location, and socioeconomic status influence the structure and organization of the self. As mentioned earlier, self-seeking moves the self into the content of human life, and mental and physical impulses constantly drive self-development.

An individual's responses to the succession of states of mind, habitual behaviors, the selectivity of the mind, and the process of attention are vital to the development of his personality (James [1892] 1985). The formation of our personalities is, in part, a response to the stimuli in our environments. Yet, we can only come to know ourselves, others, and the world from our own unique perspectives. Since each human being only has the perspective of

self, self-seeking impulses are prompted by an innate selfishness
that is informed by self-satisfaction and self-preservation—no
matter how altruistic an individual may hope to be.

Each time we encounter an idea, object, or living being, our central
nervous system responds. Once a human being encounters an idea,
object, or being, the experience alters the mind and body. Afterward,
our mental and physical states are never the same (James [1892]
1985, 21). When a sensation occurs, the brain is forever modified.
Nevertheless, as each object that appears the same repeatedly
makes an impression on the brain, it corresponds in some way to
that particular percept (1–4). With each encounter, the impressions
become more deeply ingrained in the brain. These impressions
and pathways trigger reflex actions in the nervous and muscular
systems that deepen and become more familiar (4). As we attend to
objects (ideas, people, things, places, etc.), habits are behaviorally,
physiologically, and psychologically formed. Thus, as we attend
to ourselves, or as others attend to us, the encounter stimulates
biological and mental reactions that become habitual over time.
The ingrained impressions and the habitual activities experienced
contribute to the formation of *personality* and demeanor.

This occurs as an object makes an impression upon the senses,
immediately becoming a percept within the mind. There is
movement within the body as the object changes into a percept,
leading to an alteration in the brain, nervous system, and muscular
structure. The mind and body compare the change to other changes
experienced with similar objects. With close examination, the past
and present percepts would appear different; however, thought
continues to progress in an uninterrupted fashion because of habits
and the rapidity of the thought process itself. With closer reflection,
the mind otherwise would have determined the imperfect identity

(lack of sameness). Instead, we most often confound objects and percepts, unite them together, and give ourselves the experience of what appears to be a smooth transition from one object to the next.

Either intentionally or unintentionally, we train our minds to think specific thoughts and focus attention on specific ideas, objects, and people. We create patterns of thought, and subsequently, personality evolves. As the self responds to the gestures, ideas, and objects surrounding it, mental, physical, and spiritual tensions and challenges are vital to personality formation. James holds that "He who has no solid ground to press against will never get beyond the stage of empty gesture-making" ([1892] 1985, 14). Although some habits and personality traits develop naturally, active involvement in the development of personality formation through habits and deliberate actions requires discipline and commitment to one's self and growth. The development of proper habits builds character.

The objects to which we give our attention also are important in the development of personality. It is for this reason that we must discipline and train our minds to think specific thoughts. "The longer one attends to a topic the more mastery of it one has," and gaining control of and training a wandering mind to focus on a subject "is the root of judgment, character, personality and will" (James [1892] 1985, 95). According to James, out of the mass of ideas and objects that we encounter each moment, our selective consciousness only has the ability to attend to a few. Perception of an object, brought to our attention prior to our actual encounter with it, sensitizes the mind and body to the object and equips us to attend to it when it appears (101–103). Interest plays an important role in determining the object that captures our attention. Experiences, therefore, become individualized and personalize the manner in which objects are perceived and reflected upon

([1906] 1996, 130–132). This clarifies why James, in his essay "The Self," explains that "the continuous identity of each personal consciousness as a name for the practical fact that new experiences come which look back on the old ones, find them 'warm,' and greet and appropriate them as 'mine'" (128–129).

18

The Self and Personal Identity

*T*HIS ESSAY INVESTIGATES FOUR significant issues related to the self and the theoretical and practical problems associated with the concept of personal identity. First, an analysis of the term *identity* is provided. Second is an examination of the relationship between the self and personal identity. The formation of personal identity through social relations is the third area of examination. The fourth area discusses the difference between the sameness and diversity of self. The essay concludes with summary comments.

Personal identity is a product of psychological and social processes. Reflexive awareness of past experiences plays a major role in the development of personal identity. The structure of personal identity depends upon a consciousness that extends backward into past actions and thoughts. Personal identity, therefore, depends upon the same self appearing in different places and times. Several questions arise as one thinks about personal identity: What is its basis? What role does the self play in personal identity? What is the role of social relations in personal identity?

In an essay titled "Of Identity and Diversity," appearing in *An Essay Concerning Human Understanding* (1689), John Locke struggles with the notion of personal identity. He reveals the theoretical and practical problems associated with the concept of *sameness of self*. Locke explains that identity consists of the recognition of something or someone as the same in different places or times ([1689] 1975, 328). Yet, both he and James make statements that contradict this notion. James contends that "no state once gone can recur and be identical with what it was before" ([1892] 1985, 21). Locke also asserts that

> we never find, nor conceive it possible, that two
> things of the same kind should exist in the same
> place at the same time, we rightly conclude, that
> whatever exists any where at any time, excludes all
> of the same kind, and is there itself alone. ([1689]
> 1975, 328)

How does personal identity remain consistent when people change in varying degrees from one moment to the next? A young boy matures over the course of years and becomes a man yet keeps the same identity. The veteran who loses limbs in a war maintains his identity. The actress who alters her features with cosmetic surgery holds on to her identity. A person who changes his name, character, disposition, and ideologies does so without losing his identity. What then is the basis or essence of the *sameness of person*, if it is not necessarily based upon physical characteristics, body parts, or personality?

A clear definition of the concept of *person* is necessary to unravel the problem. Locke defines a person as:

a thinking intelligent Being, that has reason and
reflection, and can consider it self as it self, the
same thinking thing in different times and places;
which it does only by that consciousness, which
is inseparable from thinking, and as it seems to
me essential to it: It being impossible for any
one to perceive, without perceiving, that he does
perceive. When we see, hear, smell, taste, feel,
meditate, or will anything, we know that we do so.
Thus it is always as to our present Sensations and
Perceptions: And by this every one is to himself,
that which he calls self. ([1689] 1975, 335)

Recognition of one's self is central to Locke's definition of a person.
Personal identity, therefore, depends upon an individual's ability
to know him- or herself as a thinking being in different places
and times. There must be awareness of the triadic relationship
occurring between the *I* and *me*, and the self must be able to reflect
upon its *own* past experiences.

But can one person access another's experiences and claim them
as his or her own? In his essay "How Two Minds Can Know One
Thing," James asks, when encountering a particular object, "Might
not two or more streams of personal consciousness include one
and the same unit of experience so that it would simultaneously
be a part of the experience of all the different minds?" ([1906]
1996, 126).

Several different minds can encounter an object, fact, or
phenomenon simultaneously. Once an object is transmitted to
the brain, it immediately becomes a percept in the mind of each
perceiver. The image is held within individual minds; sharing

between the minds, however, is impossible. A person's thoughts belong to his or her prior thoughts, while another's thoughts belong to his or her prior thoughts. The thoughts of one person never interact with those of another.

Locke dramatically questions the use of the term *identity* and wonders if the word is suited for the many concepts to which it is applied. He argues that much confusion has resulted in our misunderstanding of personal identity because of the misuse of *identity* in reference to the appropriate idea.

> 'Tis not therefore Unity of Substance that comprehends all sorts of Identity, or will determine it in every Case: But to conceive, and judge of it aright, we must consider what *Idea* the Word it is applied to stands for: It being one thing to be the same *Substance*, another the same *Man*, and a third the same *Person*, if *Person*, *Man*, and *Substance*, are three Names standing for three different *Ideas*; for such as is the *Idea* belonging to that Name, such must be the Identity. ([1689] 1975, 332)

How then can it be said that the identity of the same person, man, and substance in the same physical body is an identical self, when each idea itself is different? Locke asks:

> [Is it] not the *Idea* of a thinking or rational Being alone, that makes the *Idea* of a *Man*, the same successive Body not shifted all at once, must as well as the same immaterial Spirit go to the making of the same *Man*[?] ([1689] 1975, 335)

The substance of a person's body typically changes drastically over the course of his or her lifetime; thus, substance alone cannot be the basis of personal identity. Yet, the same continued life is communicated: (1) to different particles of matter united to that organized living body, and (2) to consciousness through reflections of thought, senses, introspection, and experience. "The Identity of the same *Man*," Locke asserts, "consists … in nothing but a participation of the same continued Life" ([1689] 1975, 331). A stream of consciousness united in one continuous life makes the same person and constitutes personal identity. Locke contends:

> For it being the same consciousness that makes a Man be himself to himself, *personal Identity* depends on that only, whether it be annexed only to one individual Substance, or can be continued in a succession of several substances …; so far it is the same *personal* self. For it is by the consciousness it has of its present Thoughts and Actions, that it is self to it self now, and so will be the same self as far as the same consciousness can extend to Actions past or to come … The same consciousness uniting those distant Actions into the same *Person*, whatever Substances contributed to their Production. ([1689] 1975, 336)

The self, that same conscious thinking thing with one life, constitutes the same person and determines personal identity. This self knows itself in the present, is aware of past actions, and is able to connect a stream of thoughts into one continuous life, which it only has experienced and continues to *feel*.

The role of other thinkers and social relations, however, cannot be overlooked as a factor in the formation of personal identity. James contends that "all we need suppose for personal identity is a succession of thinkers, each aware of the past in the same way" (Dooley 1975, 33). As a self experiences its environment and interacts with others, instantly the self transforms into a percept—like any object would—becoming a percept to him- or herself and others. The "self-turned-percept" essentially enters into his or her *own* stream of consciousness and that of others.

Like the self who appropriates past *mes* for the construction of his or her *own* personal identity, other selves also are capable of appropriating their *own* past *mes*, as well as the *mes* of others—if they experienced the same object at the same time. Each of the other selves would merely connect the *mes* of another, over a period of time, into what each considers to be the person's present *me*. Thus, just as one's own personal identity consists of a consciousness of *mes* of past experiences and the ability to recall thoughts, one's personal identity can be confirmed by others if they are aware of the *mes* of that individual in the same way. In other words, each self is a member of a group of thinking selves who are able to appropriate their own and others' past *mes*. "All that is necessary to account for knowing and the verifiable feature of personal identity is passing thought" (Dooley 1975, 34).

Memory also is required for the self to exist. Memory plays an important function in personal identity, being operative in the stream of thought and the facilitation of habits. Without memory, we would be unable to construct a self. Although our memories fail us to varying degrees, we depend upon others to recall past experiences. Such forgetfulness or dysfunction can occur because of fever, a blow to the head, disease, old age, or just an inability to hold all the happenings of life in one's mind. In cases of memory loss or an inability to visualize the past, we depend on others who have encountered the same objects to draw connections between experiences. These individuals help link us to past actions and thoughts, thereby facilitating the flow of our stream of consciousness. We each depend upon someone or something else to know our past and to confirm our existence. The interactive mechanism between the consciousness and the function of memory and their relationship with the outer world contributes to the construction of the self and formation of personal identity.

However, in his essay titled "Of Personal Identity," in *A Treatise of Human Nature*, Hume writes:

> the understanding never observes any real connection among objects ... when strictly examined, [it] resolves itself into a customary association of ideas ... [I]dentity is nothing really belonging to these different perceptions, and uniting them together; but is merely a quality, which we attribute to them, because of the union of their ideas in the imagination, when we reflect upon them ... It follows, that our notions of personal identity, proceed entirely from the smooth and uninterrupted progress of the thought along a train of connected ideas. ([1739] 1978, 259–260)

"The identity, which we ascribe to the mind of man, is only a fictitious one" ([1739] 1978, 259) asserts Hume. Like Locke, Hume contends that there is error in the manner in which the term *identity* has been and continues to be used. Hume's claim is based on the fact that we have come to believe that an object existing at one point in time is the same object existing at another. According to Hume, there is no firm foundation to the "principle of individuation," the idea upon which the self and personal identity are based, because all objects vary and are interrupted over a period of time. The error occurs when the mind holds and traces an object back over time, while assuming that it has existed without any alterations. Because of the ease of transition between the objects, we tend to erroneously accept the notion of sameness or identity instead of the concept of diversity or multiplicity (201, 251–252).

Human beings are a "collection of different perceptions, which succeed each other with an inconceivable rapidity, and are in a perpetual flux and movement ... They are the successive perceptions only, that constitute the mind" (Hume [1739] 1978, 252). Why then do we assume that a self is the same person with the same personal identity? Hume explains that this confusion arises because the term *identity* has come to imply two distinct ideas: *sameness* and *diversity*.

> We have a distinct idea of an object that remains invariable and uninterrupted through a supposed variation of time; and this idea we call ... sameness. We have also a distinct idea of several different objects existing in succession, and connected together by a close relation; and this to an accurate view affords as perfect a notion of diversity ... But though this idea of identity, and a succession of related objects be in themselves perfectly distinct, and even contrary, yet it is certain, that in our common way of thinking they are generally confounded with each other. That action of the imagination, by which we consider

the uninterrupted and invariable object, and that
by which we reflect on the succession of related
objects, are almost the same to the feeling. ([1739]
1978, 253)

We have come to experience this confusion about personal identity
and make this mistake out of habit. As mentioned in earlier essays,
impressions deepen channels in the brain and nerve centers. These
pathways facilitate the formation of habitual actions, whether they
relate to language usage, mental focus, or physical behavior. But the
development of habits is vital to human interaction; it simplifies
life by easing daily movement and facilitating the communication
process. Dr. Maudsley writes in *The Physiology of Mind*:

> If an act became no easier after being done several
> times, if the careful direction of consciousness
> were necessary to its accomplishment on each
> occasion, it is evident that the whole activity of a
> lifetime might be confined to one or two deeds—
> that no progress could take place in development.
> (James [1892] 1985, 5)

The *resemblance* between objects is another reason that we have
a propensity to make the mistake of assuming similarity between
sameness and *diversity*. Percepts that resemble one another in the
stream of thought, yet are variable and interrupted, are very easily
connected and made whole by the mind. An image of a continuous
object is transmitted. This error contributes to the problems
associated with the notion of personal identity because physical
and emotional changes in humans are most often too gradual or
incremental to alter our image of them (Hume [1739] 1987). The
confusion concerning identity is not solely based on the use of the

term; additionally, the problem also lies in the fact that we have come to believe a falsehood. We live in error, according to Hume, who says that the propensity to accept fiction as reality is absurd.

> In order to justify to ourselves this absurdity, we often feign some new and unintelligible principle, that connects the objects together, and prevents their interruption or variation. Thus we feign the continued existence of the perceptions of our senses, to remove the interruption; and run into the notion of a *soul*, and self, and *substance*, to disguise the variation. (Hume [1739] 1978, 254)

19

James's Pragmatic Self

"[F]OR RATIONALISM REALITY IS ready-made and complete from all eternity, while for pragmatism it is still in the making, and awaits part of its complexion for the future" (James [1906] 1996, 123). Pragmatism, according to James, is neither monistic nor pluralistic. It is neither optimistic nor pessimistic. While pragmatism does agree with the views of pluralism, pragmatism is melioristic. Pragmatism is oriented toward the future and posits a possibility of hope for a better world, attainable with the aid of humankind.

Human beings play a role in the expansion of knowledge in order to bring forth a better world. Through the act of joining other selves, interacting and influencing the perspectives and behaviors of one another, each self also gives attention to ideas, objects, and actions. The dynamic group of individual selves focusing their collective consciousness contributes to the growth of knowledge in the world. According to James, this process is central to the realization of a better world.

James suggests that our knowledge is incomplete. The continuing debate over truth and between truth claims proves this point. He holds that knowledge is constantly evolving; yet, he maintains that knowledge never grows all at once—instead it grows in spots. As some areas of knowledge grow, others remain unchanged. We hold on to old beliefs and opinions for stability and certainty. As knowledge is revised, however, additions occur, and both old and newly acquired opinions gradually realign themselves.

James maintains that the need for humans to hold on to old beliefs and ideas results in ancient modes of thought remaining with us today, lingering like cultural survivals and preserved retentions from generations past. These ancient modes of thought adapted themselves from one generation to the next for centuries and, according to James, form the basis for our fundamental ways of thinking, known as common sense (James [1907] 1981). Common sense provides a practical and true framework for each individual self to come to understand him- or herself through experiences.

Common sense, claims James, in practical terms means "good judgment," while in philosophical terms it means the "use of certain … categories of thought" (James [1907] 1981, 84). Each self uses categories of thought as modes to apprehend his or her experiences that come to the self as unstructured forms. These impressions are understood as we mentally classify, serialize, and connect them in systems of concepts. James asserts that there are numerous parallel conceptual systems with reciprocally related elements. To understand fully, humans must interpolate impressions into a continual chain of events. After interpolation into the mental system, we must classify impressions and draw connections from old beliefs, opinions, and experiences, while relating them to future possibilities.

Common sense, as well as many other types of thought, claim to possess the truth. Yet, James maintains, they "all seem insufficiently true in some regard" ([1907] 1981, 94). "The notion of truth," according to the pragmatist, is "the simple duplication by the mind of a ready-made and given reality" (93). The many conflicts among truth claims, however, obliges us to overhaul the very idea of truth. These conflicts should "awaken a presumption favorable to the pragmatic view that all our theories are ... mental modes of *adaptation* to reality" (94).

Truth is defined as the agreement of our ideas with reality or when our ideas copy reality. Objects and ideas and their relations must agree with concrete or abstract realities. For James, however, the most important aspect about ideas and facts agreeing with reality is not whether they are copies or symbols of reality, nor whether there is an absence of contradictory evidence in relation to a belief or idea. Most important for James is that ideas or objects help each individual to grasp, adapt to, and manage reality in order to guide himself or herself along the truth-verification process. True ideas have undergone the process of becoming true and agree with reality. The possession of truth, therefore, must not be seen as an end in itself but as "a preliminary means toward other vital satisfactions" (James [1907] 1981, 98).

For intellectualists, truth is "essentially an inert static relation." One who arrives at the truth fulfills his or her thinking destiny (James [1907] 1981, 96). For the pragmatist, truth is based on an idea's effects and the process of realizing the truth. "True ideas," the pragmatist asserts, "are those that we can assimilate, validate, corroborate and verify" (97). Contrary to the intellectualists, pragmatists believe that "the truth of an idea is not a stagnant property" (97). "Truth *happens* to an idea. It *becomes* true, is *made* true by events." The verification process for the pragmatic method is directly linked to human action and social interaction, which essentially makes truth-seeking a public activity. Each self has a responsibility to speak out and think about the other because of the communal nature of the verification process.

It is a primary duty for us to verify and validate ideas as true or false, thereby determining their usefulness or harmfulness. The objects of true ideas have relative practical importance, due to the dynamic nature of truth. Ideas are true because they are useful. "True," argues James, "is the name for whatever idea starts the verification-process, useful is the name for its completed function in experience" (James [1907] 1981, 98). The verification process allows each self to substantiate ideas as true through indirect or possible, as well as direct or actual, manifestations (105). Pragmatism does not reject any hypothesis, if useful consequences flow from it and they lead to beliefs that are useful in moving along a path towards safety or salvation. Each individual self may find universal conceptions and specific sensations usefulness and complementary to other useful manifestations in life. "The Absolute" and "one God" have proven such usefulness. Useful things help us cope with life's challenges, regulate our behaviors, and provide incentives for us to better ourselves.

The pragmatic method is based on a worthwhile progression, rising out of individual and communal experiences, where one moment or idea leads to the next. In a moment, each self is inspired with a thought. The thought guides him or her into future experiences where the thoughts and actions make connections. Truth essentially means eventual verification through a directed or guided process, based on things or relations of common sense.

Pragmatism challenges each one of us, each self, to recognize the value of the false as well as the true. It asks us not to ignore or negate the false in our attempt to recognize and affirm the truth, but to redirect our attention toward experience. Experience alters our perception of what is true. What is true today may become a falsehood or relative truth tomorrow. The beliefs we hold cause us to act, which lead to new experiences and facts that in turn challenge our understanding of ideas, objects, concepts, and relationships. Pragmatism asks each self to remain cognitively malleable because our beliefs are subsequently altered accordingly. Yet, according to the pragmatist, the process of revealing truths, falsehoods, and relative truths moves each self toward an ideal point in the future when all temporary truths converge into the "absolutely" true. Each truth, falsehood, half-truth, and relative truth makes an important contribution in the progression of the verification process (James [1907] 1981).

Since human beings desire harmony, stability, and consensus—instead of chaos, frustration, and contradiction—pragmatism allows some beliefs based on unverified truths. The pragmatist recognizes the restrictions that time and space place upon our lives, and the pragmatist understands that each self is forced to be selective and perceive things according to his or her kind. As truths are verified, a large number of unverified truths remain a part of our experience. Unverified truths, based on circumstantial evidence, provide a basis for our beliefs and are held intact as long as the untruths are unchallenged (James [1907] 1981).

Pragmatism recognizes that there are unconditional claims that must be recognized as valid (James [1907] 1981). There are claims to ideas, language, concepts, theories, and narratives that we hold unconditionally. Pragmatism also holds that we are under obligation to certain judgments by an "imperative duty" (109). We are obligated to draw upon theoretical and ideological foundations and common-sense beliefs formulated by those who came before us. These acquired systems must be recognized as valid because "True as the present *is*, the past *was* also" (103).

We have a responsibility to care about what we think about. Pragmatism holds that each self must strive for intellectual consistency and exercise care in the development of thoughts and beliefs. We are each obligated to remain loyal to the work of the individual whose mental abilities, social discourses, and communal efforts developed frameworks and systems of thought that inform thinking. Deliberate thoughts have the power to shift the patterns of one's life and collective thinking, which has the ability to bring about change in society. Earlier intellectuals—and nonintellectuals—impressed their thoughts upon their reality and subsequently affected our reality.

Pragmatists maintain that most of the beliefs we hold today are acquired from past generations. These beliefs—that were once thoughts—influence what we notice and the things to which we are sensitized. These beliefs influence the ideas, concepts, and thoughts that pique our interests and dispositions and prompt our behaviors. Yet, writes James, no matter how "fixed these elements of reality may be, we still have a certain freedom in our dealing with them" ([1907] 1981, 118). We can choose which sensations we will prioritize and upon which we will place emphasis. Our minds, through imagination and focused thought, are capable of "break[ing] the flux of sensible reality into things" (122). We include, exclude, omit, emphasize, order, and classify sensations. Selection depends on our values, interests, and dispositions, which yield different formulations of truths in various times, places, and contexts (119).

Failure to recognize these connections and maintain a commitment to acquired belief systems ultimately dislodges us from the entire system, including its truths, because truths graft themselves onto previous truths (James [1907] 1981). According to James, we are obligated not to dislodge ourselves from systems—even if the claims made are false—but to dispute and challenge untruths, thus seeking the truth through, or within, acquired systems. Just as others have lain the foundations for our belief systems, we must contribute to the belief systems that will be appropriated in the future.

In summary, James aims to humble yet empower the self by forcing each individual self to move beyond selfishness and recognize his or her mere contributions to reality. James challenges the self to take a broader perspective and respect the immense historical backdrop of beliefs, theories, and ideologies upon which he or she stands. James hopes to orient the self toward the future, to move society toward "the possible." He calls the self to be responsible to future generations and encourages the pursuit of intellectual consistency and existential curiosity as we pursue truth by drawing upon our experiences and building upon acquired theories of knowledge and systems of belief.

20

Conclusion

$\mathcal{T}$HE ESSAYS IN BOOK 3 provide a pragmatic analysis of the notion of the self. Book 3 offers a glimpse into the complex nature of the self and its material, social, spiritual, psychological, and physiological dimensions. While most of James's theories highlighted the self as a conscious, thinking, and knowing being with an eye toward the future and appreciation of the past; those of Mead focused on the self as a participant in social relations and an appropriator of values and attributes of the other and the group. For pragmatism, it is clear that the *self, personality,* and *personal identity* require both psychological and social processes to manifest.

Pragmatism views the self as the physical embodiment of conscious human activity in process in the world. It recognizes the self-seeking individual as innately reflective and purposeful as he or she reflects on the past and responds to life's challenges, while seeking ways to solve them. Despite Hume's pronouncement of fiction, in which self-aware individuals are said to live, it is clear that the pragmatic self is rooted in and rises out of experience—even if it is an absurd illusion. These experiences create for the self an environment of contrasts, stresses, and strains that contribute to evolution of the self, community, and society-at-large.

As the self engages with the objects and percepts that he or she encounters, *personality* and *personal identity* emerge. The development of intelligent, morally and socially responsible individuals, therefore, depends upon the formulation of activities and experiences that contribute to the growth of the self and the richness of society. As a member of society, the self contributes to social progress by moving with and against the forces of life—whether or not the individual is aware of his or her impact. Ideally, each self should seek to develop to his or her full potential despite the difficulties he or she may face. Only through the self-actualization of each individual self will society attain the values, structures, and social arrangements that create an environment conducive to the maturation of all selves.

21

Epilogue: Appreciating God, Ourselves, and Others

MY CHERISHED RENDEZVOUS WITH masters in the Western philosophical tradition culminated in the writing of this book. My deep appreciation for their wisdom, knowledge, and thought inspired me to engage their works in a manner that was fun, revealing, insightful, and approachable. What do I hope that you take away from this book? It is my hope that you have gained a greater appreciation for the different conceptions of God and the self in the Western philosophical tradition and how these notions of God and the self have evolved over time. I hope that this knowledge offers insights that proves to be enlightening for you. In addition to approaching the content of the philosophers' work, I also hope that their courage to self-reflect, imagine, think, create, and articulate inspires you to do the same—as their works have done for me. It is my hope that this exploration of God and the self continues to kindle a desire for self-discovery. My aim is to encourage you to become more cognitively flexible in order to break free of negative thought patterns and promote healthy thoughts and habits.

We have learned from the masters of philosophical thought that humanity benefits when we seek deeper understandings of ourselves, God, our experiences, universal laws, and our relationships with others. The philosophers in this book sought to liberate the mind from oppressive and destructive forces. Their works and projects continue to liberate us today as we face challenges—some over which we have no control. Many of these situations leave us with feelings of shame, guilt, resentment, abandonment, depression, and fear. Challenging events and circumstances should not cause us to lose hope or fail to appreciate our innate capacities to self-reflect, imagine, and create. It is these challenges that must reinforce our self-worth.

The philosophers in this work sought to help us understand who we are—our power, genius, and greatness—and our relationship with God, others, and society. By being intentional about changing our thoughts, how we perceive, what we give our attention to, and our habits and actions, we can change our perceptions of our lives and environments. In part, my aim in writing this book is to encourage the practice of cognitively flexibility to assist in pivoting from negative to positive thoughts about ourselves and lives. My aim is the promotion of healthy thoughts and habits in order to break free from negative thought patterns. We must view our conditions in life as experiences that are designed to bring us clarity and understanding about our hopes, dreams, desires, and purpose— and then muster the faith and courage to make our hopes, dreams, desires, and purpose reality. Although we may face hardships, the masters of philosophical thought assure us that God is always with us when we think about, sense, perceive, feel or imagine God.

Your life is designed to be integrated into the lives of others.

~ Dr. James P. Gills

Bibliography

Beaney, Michael. 2016. *Imagination: The Missing Mystery of Philosophy*. OpenLearn Course. England: The Open University. Available online: http://www.open.edu/openlearn/history-the-arts/culture/philosophy/imagination-the-missing-mystery-philosophy/content-section-0.

Beck, Lewis W. 1960. *A Commentary on Kant's "Critique of Practical Reason"*. Chicago: The University of Chicago Press.

_____. 1980. *Philosophical Style: An Anthology about the Writing and Reading of Philosophy*. (B. Lang, ed). Chicago: Nelson-Hall.

Cassirer, Ernst. 1951. *The Philosophy of the Enlightenment*. Princeton: Princeton University Press.

Christian, C. W. 1979. *Friedrich Schleiermacher*. Waco, TX: Word Books.

Clements, Keith W. 1991. *Friedrich Schleiermacher: Pioneer of Modern Theology*. Minneapolis: Fortress Press.

Coleridge, Samuel T. 1957. *Coleridge: Selected Poetry and Prose*. New York: Penguin Books.

_____. 1817/1975. *Biographia Literaria*. Rutland, VT: Charles E. Tuttle Co.

Descartes, René. 1637/1993. *Discourse on Method and Meditations on First Philosophy*. (Trans. Cress, D. A.) Indianapolis: Hackett Publishing Co.

Dooley, Patrick K. 1975. *Pragmatism as Humanism: The Philosophy of William James*. Totowa, NJ: Littlefield, Adams & Co.

England, Frederick E. 1968. *Kant's Conception of God*. New York: Humanities Press.

Gay, Peter. 1969. *The Enlightenment: The Science of Freedom*. New York: W. W. Norton & Co.

Gills, James P. 2004. *God's Prescription for Healing: Five Divine gifts of Healing*. Lake Mary, Florida: Siloam.

Harman, Peter M. (1983). *The Scientific Revolution*. New York: Methuen & Co.

Hicks, Esther, & Jerry Hicks. 2009. *The Vortex: Where the Law of Attraction Assembles All Cooperative Relationships*. New York: Hay House.

Hume, David. 1739/1978. *A Treatise of Human Nature*. L. A. Selby-Bigge & P. H. Nidditch (eds.). 2nd ed. New York: Oxford University Press.

_____. 1779/1990. *Dialogues Concerning Natural Religion*. M. Bell (ed.). New York: Penguin Books.

James, William. 1907/1981. *Pragmatism*. Cambridge, MA: Hackett Publishing.

_____. 1892/1985. *Psychology: The Briefer Course*. G. Allport (ed.). Notre Dame, IN: University of Notre Dame Press.

_____. 1906/1996. *Essays in Radical Empiricism*. Lincoln: University of Nebraska Press.

Kant, Immanuel. 1793/1934. *Religion within the Limits of Reason Alone*. T. M. Greene & H. H. Hudson (eds.). New York: Harper Torchbooks.

_____. 1785/1983. "Grounding for the Metaphysics of Morals." In *Ethical Philosophy*. J. W. Ellington (ed.). Indianapolis: Hackett Publishing Company.

_____. 1781/1990. *Critique of Pure Reason*. J. M. D. Meiklejohn (trans.). Buffalo, NY: Prometheus Books.

_____. 1788/1993. *Critique of Practical Reason*. L. W. Beck (trans.). New York: Macmillan Publishing Co.

Liao, Shen-yi, & Tamar S Gendler. 2011. "Pretense and Imagination." *Wiley Interdisciplinary Reviews: Cognitive Science*, 2, 79–94. John Wiley & Sons, Ltd.

Locke, John. 1689/1975. *An Essay Concerning Human Understanding*. P. H. Nidditch (ed.). New York: Oxford University Press.

_____. 1690/1980. *Second Treatise of Government*. C.B. McPherson (ed.). Cambridge, MA: Hackett Publishing Company. A public domain etext book digitized by Dave Gowan.

Mandt, A. J. 1990. *Immanuel Kant: The Giants of Philosophy Series*. Nashville, TN: Carmichael & Carmichael and Knowledge Products.

Mead, George H. 1934. *Mind, Self, & Society: From the Standpoint of a Social Behaviorist*. C. W. Morris (ed.). Chicago: University of Chicago Press.

_____. 1964. *Selected Writings: George Herbert Mead*. A. J. Reck (ed.). Chicago: University of Chicago Press.

New King James Version (NKJV) Study Bible. 1997, 2007. Nashville, TN: Thomas Nelson.

Nietzsche, Friedrich. 1887/1967. *On the Genealogy of Morals*. W. Kaufmann & R. J. Hollingdale (trans.). New York: Vintage Books.

Norton, David L. 1968. "Philosophy and Imagination." *The Centennial Review*, 12(4), 392–414. Michigan State University Press.

Palmer, Robert R, & Joel Colton. 1995. *A History of the Modern World*. New York: McGraw-Hill.

Schleiermacher, Friedrich. 1988. *On Religion: Speeches to Its Cultured Despisers*. R. Crouter (trans.). New York: Cambridge Press.

_____. 1989. *The Christian Faith*. Edinburgh, Scotland: T & T Clark, Ltd.

Staloff, Darren. 1992. *Kant's "Copernican Revolution." The Great Minds of the Western Intellectual Tradition*. The SuperStar Teachers Series (audio lectures). The Learning Company.

Sugrue, Michael. 1992. *Kant's Moral Philosophy. The Great Minds of the Western Intellectual Tradition.* The SuperStar Teachers Series (audio lectures). The Learning Company.

Tarnas, Richard. 1991. *The Passion of the Western Mind: Understanding the Ideas That Have Shaped Our World View.* New York: Ballantine Books.

Taylor, Charles. 1989. *Sources of the Self: The Making of Modern Identity.* Cambridge, MA: Harvard University Press.

Tindal, Matthew. 1730. *Christianity as Old as the Creation; or, the Gospel a Republication of the Religion of Nature.* London. Available online: https://www.preteristarchive.com/Books/pdf/1730_tindal_christianity_old_as_creation.pdf

Thomas, Nigel J T. 2004. Imagination. Dictionary of Philosophy of Mind. Available online: https://sites.google.com/site/minddict/imagination.

Toland, John. (1696). *Christianity Not Mysterious.* London. Available online: https://ia601400.us.archive.org/9/items/christianitynot00tolagoog/christianitynot00tolagoog.pdf

Warren, Robert P. 1969. *Twentieth Century Interpretation of The Rime of the Ancient Mariner.* J. D. Boulger (ed.). Englewood Cliffs, NJ: Prentice Hall.

Notes

[1] Professor Niebuhr explained in class (2/16/95) that reason includes three principal faculties:

1. The "faculty" of principles (regulative ideas of absolute unity), which is also called reason.
2. The "faculty" of understanding or application of a priori categorical rules of judgment.
3. The "faculty" of intuition or perception according to the a priori forms of time and space.

A fourth faculty was subsequently added, that being the character of parameter of reason, the drive to synthesize, i.e., the imagination.

Theoretical reason is that which systematically organizes and brings forth knowledge. See also: Beck, L. W. (1960). *A Commentary on Kant's Critique of Practical Reason*. Chicago, IL: The University of Chicago Press, 23.

[2] Kant attempts to synthesize the rationalist tradition, which says that knowledge comes from reason, and the empiricist traditions, which claim that knowledge is acquired through our senses or experiences (Beck 1960).

[3] Lecture notes. Studies in Religion and Culture: Kant, Coleridge & Schleiermacher, February 16, 1995.

4   See also: Staloff, D. (1992). "Kant's 'Copernican Revolution,'" in *The Great Minds of the Western Intellectual Tradition*. The SuperStar Teachers Series (audio lectures). The Learning Company.

Copernicus posited that the Earth was, in fact, in motion and the sun was at rest, instead of the Earth being a motionless mass around which the heavenly bodies revolved (See Tarnas 1991, 249–50). This shift in thinking opened a new way of not only looking at the world but caused a major shift in how man saw himself in the world. Kant then offered an analogous "Copernican" breakthrough in epistemology. He suggested that rather than the mind having to correspond to objects, objects must correspond to our knowledge. A priori knowledge of objects, which had not been possible, was now conceivable (Staloff 1992).

5   Staloff (1992) explains that the form of phenomena, supplied a priori by the human mind, allows sense appearances, as Kant calls them, to be arranged in certain definite relations. There are two pure forms of sensibility, called transcendental aesthetic. Kant uses the term *aesthetic* because it refers to visual representations, the form of sensibility; and the term *transcendental* because the things or forms transcend sense data and go beyond it. The two pure forms are space and time. According to Kant, said Staloff, space and time are supplied by the mind. Neither time nor space is part of the noumenal realm. Both are parts of the phenomenal realm. Time and space are ways that the mind orders all of its representations, before we are even aware of it. On this note, we have now concluded our discussion of Kant's Transcendental Aesthetic and will now move into an overview of his Transcendental Analytic.

6   Transcendental reflection, Kant explains, affords "each representation ... [a] place appointed in the corresponding faculty of cognition, and consequently the influence of the one faculty upon the other is made apparent" (Kant 1781/1990, 187). Kant then elaborates on the distinction between logical illusions, "imitation[s] of the form[s] of reason" that disappear when awakened, from

transcendental illusion, imitations of the forms of reason that continue to exist "even after [they] have been exposed" (188). The transcendental illusion occurs as a result of human cognition.

7   Kant writes: "Transcendental dialectic will therefore content itself with exposing the illusory appearance in transcendental judgments, and guarding us against it; but to make it, as in the case of logical illusion, entirely disappear and cease to be illusion, is utterly beyond its power. For we have here to do with a *natural* and unavoidable illusion, which rests upon subjective principles, and imposes these upon us as objective [principles] ... in imitation of the natural error (Kant 1781/1990, 189). "There is therefore a natural and unavoidable dialectic of pure reason ... which is an inseparable adjunct of human reason, and which, even after its illusion have been exposed, does not cease to deceive, and continually to lead reason into momentary errors, which it becomes necessary continually to remove" (189).

8   Kant writes: "In our reason, subjectively considered as a faculty of human cognition, there exist fundamental rules and maxims of its exercise, which have completely the appearance of objective principles. Now from this cause it happens, that the subjective necessity of a certain connection of our conceptions, is regarded as an objective necessity of the determination of things in themselves. This illusion is impossible to avoid... although [we are] not deceived by this illusion" (Kant 1781/1990, 188–89).

9   Kant explains his categorical imperative: "So act that the maxim of your will could always hold at the same time as the principle giving universal law" (Kant 1788/1993, 30).

10 Professor Michael Sugrue explains that Kant wanted to formulate the rules of the moral world, of moral justice and moral righteousness, to apply to things that are noumenal—the human souls, rational agents, and free entities. Thus, Kant proposed a universal law that would establish the good or evil of every action by every free, rational, moral agent, under all circumstances independent of space and time. Kant formulates the law of ultimate moral duty. He called it the categorical imperative. See Sugrue, M. (1992). *Kant's Moral*

Philosophy. The Great Minds of the Western Intellectual Tradition. The SuperStar Teachers Series (audio lectures). The Learning Company.

[11] Beck explains that Kant's notion of the comprised of the *wille* (volition), which has no incentive yet is considered the autonomous legislator, and the *willkur* (the faculty of choice), which has inherent incentive and is called the spontaneous executor (Beck 1960, 198–99).

[12] Kant, Immanuel, *Religion within the Limits of Reason Alone* (New York: Harper Torchbooks 1793/1934), xciv-xcvi. I have substituted "will" for "Willkur," the German word Kant has used in his work. Willkur "is the expression of man's transcendental freedom, his ultimate spontaneity" (xcvi). It "is determined according to the strength of the pleasures or displeasures it anticipates in connection with the alternatives open to it" (xcv). "The human Willkur [also] determines itself and is free" (xcv).

[13] See also: Kant, Immanuel. *Religion within the Limits of Reason Alone* (New York: Harper Torchbooks 1793/1934), 139.

[14] For Kant, the predisposition of man for good may be divided into three functional elements that are fundamental to man's character and destiny. They are:

(1) Animality: it may be considered a "physical and purely *mechanical* self-love";

(2) Humanity: (of a *rational* being) it reveals itself in "a self-love which is physical and yet *compares* with others" leading to jealousy and rivalry;

(3) Personality: it causes man to be "taken as a rational and at the same time an *accountable* being" who has the capacity to respect the moral law within him.

Kant also discusses man's propensity toward evil by offering three distinctive features. First, says Kant, "there is the weakness of the human heart in the general observance of adopted maxims, or in other words, the *frailty* of human nature; second, the propensity for mixing unmoral with moral motivating causes (even when it is done with good intent and under maxims of the good), that is, *impurity*; and third, the propensity to adopt evil maxims, that is the *wickedness* of human nature or of the human heart" (Kant 1793/1934, 24).

15 Kant admits that the tasks of continuously making good choices is not easy. He writes: "But in the judgment of men, who can appraise themselves and the strength of their maxims only by the ascendancy which they win over their sensuous nature in time, this change must be regarded as nothing but an ever-during struggle toward the better, hence as a gradual reformation of the propensity to evil, the perverted cast of mind" (Kant 1793/1934, 43).

16 For Kant, man as a rational, autonomous being must himself be responsible for who he becomes, and his "condition must be an effect of his free choice; for otherwise he could not be held responsible for it and could therefore be *morally* neither good nor evil," (Kant 1793/1934, 40). Man, therefore, becomes either good or evil by the free choices he makes.

17 Kant writes: "Inasmuch as virtue and happiness together constitute the possession of the highest good for one person, and happiness in exact proportion to morality (as the worth of a person and his worthiness to be happy) constitutes that of a possible world, the highest good means the whole, the perfect good" (1788/1993, 117, [111]).

18 Kant writes: "[W]herein virtue is always the supreme good, being the condition having no condition superior to it" (1788/1993, 177, [111]).

19 See: Kant 1934, Endnote 7.

20 Class notes, March 21, 1995.

21 For Kant, man as a rational, autonomous being must himself be responsible for who he becomes, and his "condition must be an effect of his free choice; for otherwise he could not be held responsible for it and could therefore be *morally* neither good nor evil" (Kant 1793/1934, 40). Man, therefore, becomes either good or evil by the free choices he makes.

22 Kant writes: "But in the judgment of men, who can appraise themselves and the strength of their maxims only by the ascendancy which they win over their sensuous nature in time, this change must be regarded as nothing but an ever-during struggle toward the better, hence as a gradual reformation of the propensity to evil, the perverted cast of mind" (Kant 1793/1934, 43).

23 As man begins to act out of sake "the predisposition is thus gradually transformed into a cast of mind, and *duty*, for its own sake, begins to have a noticeable importance in their hearts" (Kant 1793/1934, 44).

24 For Kant and Coleridge, moral value or worth is not determined by human actions but by the inner principles upon which the actions are performed; neither the actor nor the observers can, therefore, infer the intent of one's acts (Kant 1785/1983, 19, [407]).

25 As the poet, Coleridge is, in essence, the creator, thus controlling and bringing forth all life. It is Coleridge who then subjects the mariner to the endless cycle of telling his tale as penance for his guilt (Kant 1793/1934, cxxxi).

26 Upon the conclusion of reading *The Rime*, we find that the beginning of the poem is merely an entry point into a repetitive poetic cycle that is already in process. This cycle represents the mariner's adherence to a moral obligation or duty. His continuous obedience to the moral law is therefore symbolic of his transformed cast of mind (Kant 1793/1934, cxxxii).

27 Silber explains that Kant found himself holding contradictory views on his notions of inescapable guilt and the acquisition of grace (Kant 1793/1934, cxxxii, 50–53).

28 Kant admits that inescapable guilt is a concern, says Silber, because it "could lead the moral individual to despair and far greater guilt" (Kant 1793/1934, cxxxii).

29 Coleridge (1957), 54–55, lines 582–588.

30 Kant writes: "[T]he morally good disposition," i.e., the mariner's continuous telling of his story, "is nothing less than the share which such a disposition affords the rational being of legislating universal laws, so that he is fit to be a member in a possible kingdom of ends."

The mariner, therefore, has "respect" for the law. Respect for the law "alone," says Kant, "provides a suitable expression for the esteem which a rational being must have for it. Hence, autonomy is the ground of the dignity of human nature and of every rational nature" (Kant 1785/1983, 41, [436]).

31 See also: (Kant 1785/1983, 41, [447]). Here we find Coleridge's theme of the One Life; human nature and every rational being belong to a whole.

32 Kant, Immanuel, in the Introduction to *Critique of Pure Reason*. The quote was, however, taken from: Lang, Berel, "Space, Time, and Philosophical Style," in *Philosophical Style: An Anthology about the Writing and Reading of Philosophy*, ed. Berel Lang, (Chicago: Nelson-Hall, Inc. 1980), 144.

33 Class notes 4/17/95. Self-mastery involves having:

1. Power over oneself and control of circumstances
2. A proper self-attitude
3. Power to redirect one's instinct
4. Avenues to all other kinds of power one has, especially an awareness of superiority
5. An individualistic understanding of the concept, which varies from person to person
6. The will to act cruelly (a cruelty that takes over our own instincts and inclination) without an attitude of shame

Index

We hope that you have enjoyed reading *God and the Self* and have found it to be enlightening and a blessing in your life. For additional information on this book or to contact Dr. D. Pulane Lucas, please visit us at: www.dpulanelucas.com, or email us at: GodandtheSelf@gmail.com.

Printed in the United States
By Bookmasters